MORE PRAISE
FOR *RIVER SONGS*

"Fly fishing is Steve Duda's portal to the natural world. His stories are down-to-earth, passionate, and overflowing with wonder. *River Songs* is scorchingly well written."

—Peter Kaminsky, author of *Catch of a Lifetime*

"Like a fireside raconteur plucking his banjo beside your favorite stream, Steve Duda plays notes that ring true. His river songs about the angling life—about *living*—evoke a deep yearning for connection, the regret of missed opportunity, and an impatience with cheap illumination. He finds humor, absurdity, and sorrow in both the magical and the mundane. Duda's is a sometimes gruff, sometimes bemused, but always singular voice that cuts through the discordant noise of our times."

—Langdon Cook, author of *Upstream*

"Duda's tales are far more than fishing stories. They are the fatty spoils of in-between moments that only someone as unintentionally soaked in the cosmos as Duda could capture. I'm grateful for each of his experiences, in which he holds the fleeting, strange psalms long enough to translate them for mortals like me to cherish."

—Hilary Hutcheson, outfitter and guide

"As full of music and movement as a river, Steve Duda's *River Songs* is for the soul of every fly fisher. The still-water of this generous collection: contemplation. The punk-rock rapids: a rollicking good time. The nicks and dings, the smooth keel: like the best writing of all, there are stories, images, and metaphors here that will carry you away and make your life richer for the journey."

—Cameron Keller Scott, author of *Watershed*

"Fly-fishing has changed since we baby boomers were young and we're not always happy about it, so it was a relief to open Steve Duda's *River Songs* and find an entirely recognizable world where all the familiar traditions are alive and well, including that of compelling stories told with skill and intelligence."

—John Gierach, author of *Trout Bum*
and *All the Time in the World*

"What strikes me most about these inviting and enjoyable stories is their authenticity. Duda writes—and I mean this in the best way—like he has dirt under his fingernails."

—Monte Burke, author of *Lords of the Fly* and *Saban*

RIVER SONGS

MOMENTS OF WILD WONDER IN FLY FISHING

STEVE DUDA

MOUNTAINEERS BOOKS

 **MOUNTAINEERS BOOKS** is dedicated to the exploration, preservation, and enjoyment of outdoor and wilderness areas.

1001 SW Klickitat Way, Suite 201, Seattle, WA 98134
800-553-4453, www.mountaineersbooks.org

Printed in Canada
27 26 25 24   1 2 3 4 5

Design and layout: Jen Grable
Illustrations: Matthew DeLorme
Page 171: "Drinking Fisherman" photo courtesy of Historic Photo Archive, historicphotoarchive.net.

Library of Congress Cataloging-in-Publication Data is available at https://lccn.loc.gov/2024004673. The ebook record is available at https://lccn.loc.gov/2024004674.

Mountaineers Books titles may be purchased for corporate, educational, or other promotional sales, and our authors are available for a wide range of events. For information on special discounts or booking an author, contact our customer service at 800-553-4453 or mbooks@mountaineersbooks.org.

♻ Printed on 100% recycled and FSC-certified materials

ISBN (hardcover): 978-1-68051-701-9
ISBN (ebook): 978-1-68051-702-6

An independent nonprofit publisher since 1960

FOR LORI,

MY CONFIDANT, COMPANION, AND CO-CONSPIRATOR

¡SIEMPRE MEJOR!

*"The only people who inveigh
against escape are jailers."*

—J. R. R. TOLKIEN

CONTENTS

LESSONS

Fly fishing teaches us a few things about a few things. We know which way is north and which direction the winds blow when the weather's about to turn. We can stop the bleeding, patch the leaks, and always have duct tape handy. We know a few good knots, a few good jokes, and can curse in a handful of languages. We can pitch a tent in the dark and point to a few constellations. We know how to ford a river, build a fire, and brew a cup of coffee. We can open a beer with almost anything.

We're good sports and gracious winners who are used to long odds and making friends with failure. We're blessed with a vast reservoir of hope and we trust that better outcomes and brighter prospects—the next cast, the next run, the next day—are around the next bend.

We're a family of enthusiastic activists, weirdos, obsessives, and odd-balls exploring the peculiar back alleys, sidetracks, and secret rooms of our sport. Fly fishing isn't just one thing; it's a whirling ball of bamboo rods, blue-lining, and bass. It's poetry, permit, and plotting to bring down dead-beat dams. It's tarpon, tenkara, and the alchemy of old fishing caps. It's carp, conservation, and keeping a cigar lit in a sideways gullywasher. It's steelhead, shore lunches, and the beauty of native fish. It's strange and beautiful—beautifully strange—and it's what we do.

Most of all, this is a family that understands and appreciates the enormity, wildness, and wonder of the outdoors. Together, we stand in its light with humility, appreciation, and the determination not to lose what we love.

When you try to explain these things, they might sound silly or absurd or a waste of time. But more than anything, we understand that having a compass, knowing which way the wind blows, and finding shelter from a storm count for something. And if a ridiculous activity like fly fishing can help us to be a generous friend, point us toward excellence, and encourage a profound and abiding love for this planet, then spending time sitting on a riverbank watching clouds pass overhead seems to be an excellent way to spend our days. That lesson is as real as it gets.

1

GHOSTS

"When the buffalo are gone we will hunt mice, for we are hunters and we want our freedom."

—SITTING BULL

Come early summer, Washington State's Columbia Basin is a griddle. Heat wobbles everything. Wind sandblasts paint off abandoned farm equipment, and red-tailed hawks ride upswelling thermals for hours, looking for something—anything—to rustle the sage. Despite the inhospitable nothingness, the sweet smell of mint carries on the wind. There are apple stands along the melting two-lane asphalt roads. Trucks loaded with sugar beets regularly rumble past. Since 1948, the Columbia Basin Project has been siphoning what equates to the annual flow of the Colorado River from the once-mighty Columbia to slake the thirst of the vineyards, orchards, and hop vines that paint what should be a dusty brown canvas in huge, regularly irrigated green circles and rectangles. Nothing fragile should grow here, but thanks to the metronomic *click-click-click* of the center pivot and the sputtering snake-hiss of wheel-line irrigation systems, it does.

We plot trips to this desert only when it's decided it's simply too damn hot to fly fish for trout a few miles away. After all, who wants to jolt-jump over the Yakima Canyon's ornery crew of northern Pacific rattlesnakes, and then broil on a casting deck slinging flies to overheated, sluggish red-band rainbows, when, instead, we could death-march along the scorching Columbia, posthole through knee-high, foul-smelling muck, and pitch to indifferent, skittish carp that may or may not even be there in the first place?

The Columbia, of course, once hosted history's most prolific salmon runs. Archeological evidence tells us the fish have been harvested here for at least ten thousand years, nourishing thriving, sustainable civilizations. Salmon are everywhere—and are everything—to the Native cultures along the Columbia and her tributaries. From creation stories to art to commerce to the regeneration of the land and spirit, this is salmon country, and those of us who live here are—we flatter ourselves—still salmon people. This water's true name is Nch'i-Wàna—Great River.

When the Lewis and Clark Expedition began its drift toward the Pacific in the autumn of 1805, William Clark noted that "the rivers were crouded with salmon." Indeed, "the number of dead salmon on the shores and floating in the river is incredible to say." Ask any old-timer about the runs before Roosevelt's dams started going up in the 1930s, and you'll hear the old chestnut about being able to promenade across the Nch'i-Wàna on the backs of the salmon and never soak your boots.

The sad collapse of this once-teeming abundance has been well documented. Careless environmental practices, overfishing, resource extraction, failed hatchery remediation, and inefficient, pitiless dams conspired to bully salmon populations into free fall. Our present spectral returns are a seasonal reminder of a shortsighted hubris as awe-inspiring as the vast, lonely spaces that this flow once dominated. Nothing symbolizes this tragedy more than the events of April 29, 1955. On that day, the Oregon Historical Society turned up at a small village along the Columbia with a moving camera and a reporter to document the Feast of the First Salmon. For Celilo Falls, the site of a diverse, thriving Tribal community and one of North America's oldest continually occupied sites, the feast was usually a day of celebration and ecstatic connection with the earth. On this warm and blustery spring day, however, it was a wake. It would be the final ceremony before the falls, its scaffolded fishing stations, and its small village were submerged by the backwaters of the Dalles Dam.

There is a nineteen-minute film documenting the events. It is easy to find on the internet. The ceremony is captured from a clinical remove. Each ritual, dance, and movement are flatly described, and the camera is left to linger awkwardly on the scene—intrusive, out of context, banal. Its grainy, black-and-white footage is accompanied by scratchy soundtrack that makes it seem like it was recorded centuries ago. The voice-over narration is as dry as dead leaves and painfully elides the tragedy playing out on the film. As the herky-jerky recording captures the sad scene, the narrator intones, "Though the Indians live modestly, their hospitality is lavish."

By early 1957, the gates of the Dalles Dam were closed and Celilo Falls—the narrowing of the great river where Umatilla, Klickitat, Walla Walla, Cayuse, Nez Perce, Yakama, Warm Springs, and other Tribes had fished, traded, and convened since before time was counted on calendars—was swallowed up forever. "Once this was our land, and Celilo was our falls," remarked Flora Thompson, wife of Wyam Chief Tommy Thompson. "Now our lands and our fishing places are gone, and soon we will be gone, too. Once we were many. Now we are few."

Today, we are left with *Cyprinus carpio*, the rather glumly designated common carp. The regret, accusations, and handwringing trotted out when the Columbia's ghost salmon are mentioned are matched only by the contempt for our current quarry. When the subject is raised, carp are usually on the receiving end of eradication programs, crossbows, or quarter sticks of dynamite. Among fly anglers, however, there is love enough. The common carp has been recast as the fabled basalt bonefish, the wily and elusive Columbia River brownback, the rod-busting desert ditch pig.

Unlike salmon and steelhead, wild creatures requiring an ocean's worth of space to grow, carp took quickly to domestication, which happened more or less simultaneously across the globe. In the fifth century CE, a Chinese businessman named Fan Li wrote instructions for raising them in ponds. Around the same time, well-to-do Romans grew them in specially constructed pools. For the Romans, carp was considered a delicacy fit for feasting, served roasted, boiled, or pickled and accompanied by oysters, pheasant, peacock, and slabs of bread, all helped down the gullet by cups of watered-down red wine.

Carp fishing was mentioned by Sir Izaak Walton in 1653. He writes in *The Compleat Angler*, "The Carp is the queen of rivers; a stately, a good, and a very subtle fish; that was not at first bred, nor hath been long in England, but is now naturalized." Carp fishing is still a very big and very serious deal in the United Kingdom. There are multiple magazines detailing hundreds of techniques and selling thousands of pieces of gear, all aimed at snagging a big-bellied carp wallowing in a pay-to-play lake fishery.

It was an anonymous Oregonian who, in 1880, set himself up with a few dozen carp imported from Germany, a handsome new spawning pond on the banks of the Columbia, and lofty dreams of menus featuring carp caviar, jellied carp, carp soup, and thick carp steaks. These finned pioneers were hardly "common." According to the surviving narrative, the vanguard that begat the Columbia River population were, according to a surviving account, "genuine German carp and perfect beauties." Within a year, the brood grew to more than seven thousand fish. That spring, however, disaster struck. A never-ending Northwest deluge caused the pond to overflow and fail, sending the beauties finning into the Columbia. Finding a happy home in the river, the exceptionally adaptable carp did what they do best: they bred quickly and frequently, and they got big—fast. By the turn of the twentieth century, Columbia carp were being harvested in massive numbers and used as fertilizer for farmers. The cost: five bucks a ton.

A few years ago, for about twenty minutes, fly fishing for carp was the hot new thing in the United States. Perhaps it was because of the hostility heaped upon the fish due to their homely looks and brutish ways that they became the anti-heroes—the punk-rock bonefish—of the fly fishing world. The hype didn't last. Most fly anglers went back to their trout streams because the truth is, carp can be as tricky to hook as permit; they ain't all that easy to find and, once hooked, well, then what?

Every carp expedition begins with recon. But because carp anglers are conspiratorial and secretive, reliable information is always remarkably difficult to come by. Dam-release schedules are studied, water temps verified, and a single, trusted contact residing near the flats is gently prodded/bribed for firsthand intel. Mostly, we go by our guts. Does the forecast call for hot, hotter, hot as hell? Will the winds be calm? Will the water be low enough to expose the stalking grounds?

Columbia River carp flourish in the wide spots between the hated dams. What was once described by cold, tumbling runs and broad, sweeping pools stuffed with salmon is today a tepid, featureless, barely moving reservoir pinched between the United States Army's Yakima Training Center firing range on one side and row after row of apple trees and prefab housing on the other.

To get to the carp flats from Seattle, cross the Columbia at Vantage and head south. Drive past the cherry stands near Beverly, the taco trucks at Mattawa, and the wineries at the base of the Saddle Mountains until you see the post that formerly held the sign pointing to where the public fishing access used to be. Take a sharp right and skirt the destroyed single-track to the river. Shift into 4x4 mode and follow the trace along the bank. Park out of sight, in the shade. Drink some water and enjoy a last moment of air-conditioned comfort in your truck. It's about to get hot.

Carp creep onto the river's flats—broad expanses of clear, knee-high water that shelter and nourish vast underwater fields of clams—when the sun is high and the water warm. When you walk across the flats to an exposed island two hundred yards offshore, the shells crunch underfoot. The bottom is riddled with pockmarks caused by the rooting snouts of big, hungry fish sucking up the bivalves. It's impossible to miss the areas where carp have been. The river bottom looks like a lunar surface, riddled by a meteorite storm.

There are many theories when it comes to fly selection. Wooly buggers, everyday trout nymphs such as pheasant tails and hare's ears, bonefish flies, and crawfish patterns have all been known to work. Most carp anglers prefer self-styled creations—quick-sinking, nymph-shaped inventions with just enough movement (a whiff of rabbit tail, a shock of marabou) to catch the eye of a gorging carp.

Anglers wade deliberately across the flats. Everyone looks as if they are in slow motion, and their profiles shimmer in the unrelenting heat as they drift farther and farther apart. Carping is a sight-fishing activity, and when one is spotted, the game has just begun. If the carp is a cruiser, swimming with the targeted purposefulness of a deep-water submarine, forget it. Let it swim by. Cruisers don't eat, and eaters ain't cruising. Spot one with a nose pressed to the riverbed, tail swishing the air, and a small puff of mud discoloring the water nearby–and then, well, maybe . . .

Are you close enough? Forty-foot casts just don't cut it on the carp flats. You need to see the carp inhale the fly. Creep closer. Peel some line. Measure—not too many false casts. No line whipping over the target. No sudden movements. No crossing shadows. No overhead birds. No sloppy casts. Place the fly. Gently. Yes. There.

A carp can suck up a fly from a surprising distance, and a strike telegraphs a weighty, dull thump through the line. More than likely, the fly is lodged in the carp's thick, rubbery lip. It's not coming out until your tippet breaks, the rod snaps, or you land the fish.

A carp's initial run is like a logging truck chugging down a steep grade. At first, it's not rolling that quickly, but good luck getting it under control and forget about stopping it anytime soon. A heavy basalt bone of about twelve to fifteen pounds will run one hundred yards before taking his first breather. Expect another handful of spirited efforts before surrender. Cradle the carp under the belly and remove the fly. Revive. Repeat. It will take a few moments to catch your breath while you swab carp slime off your clothes with tepid river water.

There are only a few hours of prime fishing. The winds inevitably whip down the canyon, chopping the flow and conspiring with the declining sun's glare to end your ability to see into the water. It's over. No sense in even attempting to spray casts, hoping for a Hail Mary. It won't work.

Back at the truck, after a cold can of beer, it's time to resurrect the river's ghosts—the salmon. No matter how good the day's carp fishing was or wasn't, we'll abandon the carp post-game analysis in favor of commemorating the salmon. What it must have been like way back when—before the dams? How big the runs must have been; how good the fishing surely was; how we've been cheated, deprived, and robbed of our true fish. We'll silently nod our heads and spit into the dirt as we invoke yet another description of the phantoms to which we are shackled.

Of course, we'd rather be fishing the Nch'i-Wána for steelhead and salmon. Who wouldn't? The point is, we aren't. We can't. No one home. No forwarding address. Only these haunting spirits—unavoidable, ever-present, contemptible. We are witnesses to a never-ending eulogy. We are left with only the comfort of our indignation. We are left with *Cyprinus carpio*.

These are our ghosts, as much a measure of carping as the carp themselves.

Impossibly Violent and Savagely Fast

My heart was pounding and my hands were shaking. He smelled like cucumbers—cucumbers splashed with lemon. I had him under the belly and by the tail, pointing him toward the camera. He flashed teeth as drops of bloody saltwater fell from his gills onto the fiberglass deck of the skiff. Barracuda—the big ones—leer as if they've done something depraved and wicked, and quite enjoyed the wickedness and depravity.

This was an oversized Bahamian flats predator, and our guide, Sizzle, wanted to take it home. He sprang down from the poling platform and grabbed the fish under the gills, holding it away from his body like an unexploded munition. He wrestled it to the deck and in a few seconds, the business was done. I didn't watch what sounded like a 2x4 smacking a cinder block.

It's easy to assign terrible motives to barracuda. They are chaos agents, berserkers, marauders—the most maniacal things that roam the flats. They attack by ambush, and their judgments are fast and final. These traits are not their fault, but they eat a lot of bonefish, and, according to Sizzle, they're delicious—slightly sweet with an undercurrent of ocean umami funk.

The barracuda destroyed an eight-inch chartreuse popper at 12:14 on a Tuesday afternoon. The flats were glassy. There was almost no wind. The weather was just getting sticky.

The fish was in three feet of water—not moving, just finning—waiting. The take was impossibly violent and savagely fast. On the boat, we all yelped a little.

The first run was short and punctuated by a three-foot leap. The rage was terrifying. The second run was a torpedo pointed directly at the boat. It was a long shot, but what if the next jump landed the barracuda in the skiff? Three-and-a-half feet of slashing razor wire ripping at sunburned calves, a whirlwind of apex-predator scalpels desperate for something to sever. We crouched instinctively and yelped again.

By 12:36, the entire scene had played out. The barracuda no longer smelled of cucumbers and lemons. The grin was still wicked, the drying skin pulling taut the flesh around his dagger teeth. His eyes had started to fade, but the dead stare made his gaze all the more creepy and unsettling—as if he were still capable of mayhem. We sat there in silence for a few moments—taking it all in, catching our breath—then got back to fishing.

At the dock the following morning, Sizzle slipped me a foil package. "It's your 'cuda," he said. The deep-fried chunk smelled like coconut oil and black pepper.

Barracuda are not considered safe to eat. Due to their diet high on the food chain, they store a substance called ciguatoxin in their flesh. The larger the 'cuda the more ciguatoxin, and there's no way to tell if a particular fish carries the poison or not. It's tasteless, doesn't smell, and cooking the fish doesn't kill it. If you consume a carrier, you have a chance of contracting ciguatera. There is no cure for ciguatera poisoning, which will bombard your gastrointestinal, neurological, and cardiovascular systems for anywhere from two days to a month, provoking symptoms that include vomiting, loose bowels, vertigo, heart problems, numbness, and even hallucinations.

I thought about the leering 'cuda, about how dangerous he looked, how evil I supposed him to be, his fury, his teeth, that malicious grin. I unwrapped the foil package and noticed my hands were shaking. I put a piece in my mouth.

2

MAKE THE
SKY BETTER

A Meditation on the Western Cliff Swallow

"True hope is swift and flies with swallow's wings."
—WILLIAM SHAKESPEARE

My friend Lang once hooked a cliff swallow during the annual bug blizzard that is the Mother's Day caddis hatch on the Yakima River in central Washington. As the bugs ascended from the bottom of the river, the swallows descended from their mud nests along the canyon's basalt walls. The trout noticed the bugs and began to slurp up the stragglers caught in the film. In an instant, a blustery, slow-moving spring afternoon on the water was transformed into a dramatic and frantic feeding session. Fluffy, billowing clouds of caddis, swooping birds, slashing trout, and hopeful anglers—we all met on the river's surface. The bugs were looking for love, the trout and the swallows were looking for a meal, and we were there to witness, and perhaps if everything went according to plan, fool one of those trout with a wisp of elk hair, the tip of a rooster feather, and a few inches of tinsel tied to a hook—a crafty, productive, and time-tested imitation.

Suddenly, Lang yelled something that was not quite speech—a sort of choked-back holler that couldn't entirely escape his mouth. I turned from my casting to look as a tiny swallow cartwheeled wildly into the bank, still very much attached to the line. My heart sank, and I stood in the water dumbly. A swallow? Please, no. Anything but a swallow.

On the river, anglers spend more time gazing upon swallows than upon any other creature. They are our constant, delightful companions. In the Yakima Canyon—and on any trout stream in the American West—deer, elk, moose, eagles, hawks, otters, dippers, mink, kingfishers, snakes, and field mice may take short curtain calls, but it's the swallow who's always on stage, always front and center, always entertaining. Fish may be rising to gulp bugs, other lesser birds may be squawking and crying, clouds will come together and pull apart in entrancing combinations, but it's the swallows that mesmerize. It's the swallows that never fail to lift our hearts.

On the river and off, we've shamelessly convinced ourselves that we share the best qualities with these birds. Swallows alight in us thoughts of freedom, of course, but also inspire the notion of a brilliant nonattachment—a care-free, in-the-moment appreciation for the now that might make a Buddhist monk smile from atop his meditation cushion.

For such small animals—a chubby swallow only just approaches an ounce—they inspire grand thoughts and warm feelings. Their unbridled display of pure joy and their openhearted loyalty to a piece of water and its seasons inspires the same feelings in us. Just the sight of them signifies a homecoming, a returning year after year, a sense of kinship to our friends and the earth. We don't have to be told that in art, religion, and myth, swallows have symbolized these things for centuries. We know it instinctively, just by gazing upon them.

Swallows are on the river for the bugs and, we'd like to imagine, for the sheer, ecstatic delight of simply being under the sun. We, too, are there for the bugs, the trout, and—like the swallows—the pure thrill of just being there. And it's the simple delight of stopping fishing, stopping hiking, stopping everything, and watching the swallows that adds a sweetness to the surroundings that, if only for a moment, allows us to taste and share their joy. Just by being there, swallows make the river better, make the sky better, make us better.

Lang clambered to the bank, pulled himself out of the water, and, in a single motion, flung his rod down while grabbing the line where it lay on the ground. As he scrambled over craggy basalt boulders, he held the line above his head and let it slip through his fingers, guiding him toward the swallow, about fifty feet up the bank, where it was desperately attempting to lift off and failing, failing, failing.

I shouldered out of the water, pushing through reeds and cattails, beelining to where the bird, now on a short tether, performed her sad and desperate dance. Lang and I arrived at the bird together. Our duty was clear: calm and then attempt to free the poor bird. The catching had been easy—a mistake. The bird had simply snatched Lang's fly, and that was that. She was hooked. Now, the release part would be tricky and maybe fatal. I looked at Lang. As he was saying, "Jacket!" I was already peeling it off. I edged near and tossed it over the bird. Everything fell still. I tried to gulp air and realized this was as close to a swallow as I'd ever been. The silence was horrible.

There are nearly ninety species of *Hirundinidae*, a classification family including swallows, martins, and saw wings. They are found on all continents— even Antarctica when the weather is right. All swallows have one thing in common—they hunt insects on the wing, plucking them out of the air or skimming the river's surface to snatch them from the film. Evolution has gifted them with slender, streamlined bodies and long, pointed wings, allowing for remarkable maneuverability and endurance. Because their bodies are so well suited for the job, they are highly efficient fliers and gliders. They make it look easy because it *is* easy for them. The metabolic rate of swallows in flight is half to three-quarters slower than that of a sparrow or finch—birds that are roughly the same size.

Because there are so many different types of swallows in the world, there are many ways to name them. Depending on where your swallows live, they can, en masse, be called a flight, a gulp, a swoop, a herd, or a richness. These names all seem remarkably charming and perfectly selected, as if the swallows had picked them out themselves.

On the Yakima River, a swoop of two hundred swallows may be cavorting above the flow as I stand in the middle of a run, casting away, but even that close I still strain to hear them over the gentle rush and gurgle of the tumbling water. No shrieks of joy, no jealous guarding of territory, no cries of warning—only sometimes do we hear the whispering *chirp-chirp-click-click*, their voices joined like hundreds of tiny stone bells chiming in a temple garden. For a creature that seems so bursting with joy, they remain enigmatically quiet, apart and to themselves. The emotions we've assigned to them are expressed almost wholly in a delicate physicality that seems barely bound by the laws of gravity.

Was she fatally injured? About to die? We didn't know—yet. Was there some sort of terrible cosmic penalty for killing a swallow? I was almost sure there was—there had to be. The gods, karma, fate—whatever—would not cotton to this sort of reckless destruction. Swallows are certainly one of creation's favorite beings. If she died there on the banks of the Yakima River, there would be hell to pay.

According to Christian folklore, swallows circled the cross as Christ was being crucified, plucking the spikes from his crown of thorns. They gained their iridescent sheen, the legend says, when a drop of blood fell from his wounds onto the birds' heads and chests. The swallow's annual reappearance in the spring is said to symbolize the resurrection of the Savior. They even get a mention in the book of Psalms, where they are known as "birds of freedom."

In the Egyptian Book of the Dead, swallows were known as the "imperishable stars"—heavenly bodies near Earth's poles that never seem to rise or set. The duty bestowed upon these small, flickering creatures was to slip the bounds of the physical world and usher the dead to their eternal home in the afterlife.

When sailing ships dominated the high seas, the birds were assigned a similar task. It was said that they descended from the heavens to escort a drowned sailor's soul to his eternal reward. Swallows stick close to land, so spotting a bird on the wing while voyaging was good news. When a swallow was glimpsed, home, safety, and family were all near. Owing to these good and generous deeds in the service of seamen, a sailor could earn a swallow tattoo inked high up on the neck, chest, or upper arms (to ensure the bird's unobstructed, lofty view) only after five thousand miles at sea. A second could only be added after a mere five thousand miles more. Despite the ubiquity of swallows tattooed across hipster biceps, shoulders, and necks today, they were once hard to get and precious to hold.

There is no corresponding mythology in fly fishing that promises swallows will perform the same role should a fly angler find himself lodged in a sweeper, blasted by lightning, tossed into the outboard, or otherwise drowned. This may explain why fly anglers have zero traditions involving stylized representations of the bird permanently inked into the skin. It's a shame—if any group owes homage to the swallow, it's us.

I stood next to Lang feeling shock and shame and utter confusion over what to do next. The jacket rustled. It seemed to intensify the desperation of the scene. "Jesus, man, do something," I said.

"Okay. Okay," Lang said, "Here we go." He knelt next to the jacket, reaching his hands under, feeling for the line first, then the bird.

"I've got the tippet."

I inched closer and looked around. Had any other anglers witnessed this? Had any other swallows?

"Now I've got the bird. I've got her!"

I stood by. There was nothing helpful I could offer unless useless, unsolicited advice had suddenly become helpful.

"Be careful, man. Please don't hurt her. The wings . . . be careful of her wings."

Humans have always been fascinated by the flight of birds—not simply the flight, but the idea of flight. Oh! to beat gravity and take wing on a breezy summer afternoon. To see the river from the soaring vantage of an osprey, to glide through its corridors like a heron, to noisily claim ownership of a small corner of it like a kingfisher or a red-winged blackbird. But to describe what happens when a swallow takes wing is to condense our dreams of flight and firecracker them in a shower of iridescence. What a swallow can do in the air is not merely flight; it is an impossibility made physical. The turns, the dives, the speed, the endless games of chase. If we equate flight to joy, the swallows must be laughing all the time.

Lang's face was unmoving. He was biting his lower lip so hard it had turned entirely white. I stood over his shoulder, feeling as helpless as I ever have. "Okay, I've got the hook. Jesus, I hope I pinched that goddamn barb." He turned his head and grunted. Time seemed to stop. My teeth were clenched. My fists were white-knuckled balls of aluminum foil bound in barbed wire.

"Okay, it's out," Lang rasped. "Leave the jacket on for now. I want to see if she's okay."

We were trapped there like that, Lang on his knees, his hands cupping the bird covered by the jacket, and me standing over them with nothing to do but fret and stew and hope.

I have always wondered what it would be like to hold a swallow. If your heart could keep from bursting, would the experience be remarkable or horrible? Would you note her shimmering glow, her weight, the color of her eyes? Would you, somehow, attempt to feel the very life of and in her? But would that be a quick glimpse of wonder, or would it be a horrible offense against the wind? Would your heart leap at the beauty of the creature, or would it recoil from the fact that for a man to hold a swallow seems to insult both the bird and the sky—their sky—from which she was plucked?

"I guess she's okay . . . I mean, I can't tell. She's moving, at least. She's not dead."

"Well, let's let her go."

There was nothing else we could think to do. We had either murdered this bird and were about to be cursed for all time, or the little swallow had somehow survived her hooking, crash landing, and impromptu surgery. I inched the makeshift tent from over the bird. Lang held the swallow next to the earth. On his knees, his face to the ground, it looked like he was praying. We were both praying. Slowly, he opened his cupped hands, and the bird lifted magically away, flying upstream, downstream, high, low, and in between—as if testing the flight controls—free again.

Untethered from gravity, swallows belong neither to the earth, the air, or the water, but exist as something between the elements—a magical filament that binds them together. We rarely see a swallow on the ground, and in flight, they're not satisfied to merely flap their wings and glide around. They are compelled to dive from great heights, swooping, describing curlicues and filigrees, skimming the water, and only barely brushing it with the tips of their wings as they easily pick off the fattest mayfly zigzagging above the stream.

To a swallow, the earth is a mere springboard. The wind is for tricking. The water is for teasing. Swallows are not content to just swim through the sky; they swim through the sky to make the sky better.

———

Lang was visibly shaken and seemed both elated and humbled at the bird's release. I felt relieved, of course, but also exhausted.

The swallow, Lang said, was utterly weightless, and the only thing that could be felt was the heart beating. "Whose heart?" I asked him.

"Both," he said. "Hers. Mine. For that one second, I could just feel a single heartbeat."

RIVER SONG

A Long Run with a Tight Crew

I'd been crying for a couple of hours when my phone dinged, announcing a new message. "She had a long run with a tight crew," it read. "She was a hell of a fishing dog. Thinking of you and sending love. Take care of yourself. Hugs."

I turned off the phone and stared out the window. It was 39 degrees outside. It had been raining for seventeen days straight in Seattle. It was 9:53 on a Tuesday morning and I already wanted to erase the day. My semi-feral golden retriever, Gibby, had been overwhelmed by a ruthlessly sudden illness. The vet had just put her down. My best friend of fifteen years. Gone.

I opened a beer and thought about the note. Gibby certainly had a long run with a tight crew, but she was far from a hell of a fishing dog. Like you and me, she had her quirks. She had some issues.

I was always proud to boast about how she'd once won a fight with a Yakima Canyon rattler, but she also lost battles with porcupines, skunks, raccoons, and ticks. One evening, after a tromp through the eastern Washington desert looking for a bass pond, I picked more than a hundred bloodsuckers from her hide. She loved the attention and thought the whole thing was a bonding moment.

Land battles aside, when the water wasn't too deep, she'd always wade out with me to get in on the fishing. If it was cold, she'd hang near the bank, shiver, and crawl up in the reeds, making herself as small as a seventy-five-pound dog could. If it was broiling hot, she'd lap river water, belch, and find a shallow spot in the shade to relax. No matter what, she'd always keep an eye on the fly as it drifted down the river. Gibby knew what was supposed to happen, and when it did, she'd trot to my side to inspect and congratulate me, smiling up at me as if we were both in on the same joke.

Gibby was far too enthusiastic to be graceful. More times than I can count, I watched her bob down the river, swept downstream lord only knows how far. On her way back upstream, she'd find something dead to roll in.

She loved walking with me along the tracks that ran through our favorite river canyon. She'd let me know when a train was coming or a rattler was around. Occasionally, we would flush a bird, both of us pretending we weren't startled but chuckling over our tiny, excited leaps.

I'll admit it—Gibby was overly friendly. Other dogs thought she was too forward. Other anglers thought she was poorly mannered. She was an aggressive licker and loved to bark for the sake of barking. She would balance on the bow of my raft, howling at other anglers as we bobbed downstream. Sometimes they'd flub their casts or glare at us. All of this was probably my fault, but we both thought it was hilarious.

She once ate an entire box of steelhead flies and seemed to enjoy the texture.

She was a lousy bird hunter. She just didn't get it, and I think she preferred a breezy day goofing off beside the river. Fishing was more leisurely, more unrestrained, and she had fewer responsibilities.

She was a hoarder of dog toys and tennis balls, and hid her secret stash in her hangout by the shady back corner of the garden. Her favorite was Baby, a mini version of herself, a small stuffed golden retriever with a goofy smile.

Gibby loved bullshitting around campfires and would check in with everyone before prowling the perimeter, knocking over beer bottles and lapping up the spilled prize.

She snored when she was drunk.

She won a few unsanctioned, all-breed dog races. She was warm on freezing nights and was never shy about chatting up strangers at boat launches, grocery-store parking lots, and campgrounds.

Thinking of Gibby now, the fishing part seems like a small slice of a huge memory pie. What's really important is the part about a long run with a tight crew. Loyalty. Friendship. A shared life. Now that a furry portion of it is gone, that crew means even more to me.

Love is hard to define. Words get in the way of understanding it. With a dog, love is a simpler thing. It's as easy as sharing a streamside sandwich, being generous with hugs, and always keeping a couple tennis balls handy. With our friends, it can be more complex. But just say it. Tell someone you love them and that you feel lucky to be a part of their tight crew.

DETROIT

BENNETT

3
SLIDE!

I bounded through the stadium's front gates with my old man. I had my mitt. I had my lucky cap. I had just finished a hot dog with mustard and onions served up by a wisecracking vendor in the parking lot. I was relishing the thought of my two brothers back home. They'd be staring into the TV—glazed and rendered motionless by pure, jealous rage.

I was a devoted baseball fan by age five, and finally getting to march through the turnstiles, "at the corner of Michigan and Trumbull" for the very first time put me on tiptoes, all senses afire. We ran up the long ramps outside the stadium, my pop barely able to keep me tethered. At last, there before me—the grand old ballyard. Tiger Stadium. I will never forget the glowing green field, the space defined by the bleachers, the dirt, the scoreboard, the smell. Everything came on at once. It was the first time I remember being overwhelmed, awestruck, filled with wonder. I stood there taking in a gorgeous baseball box canyon as my beloved Detroit Tigers lined up along the first-base line, hats in hand for the national anthem.

Baseball has been played at "The Corner" since 1895. The club's original owner, George Vanderbeck, tacked up some wooden stands in an old Irish neighborhood named Corktown. He called the ballyard Bennett Park, named after Charlie Bennett, a tough-as-nails catcher who played for the Detroit side—then known as the Wolverines—from 1881 to 1888. Known for his staunch defense, rocket arm, and consistent bat, Bennett had a solid career bursting with interesting trivia. He's credited with inventing the catcher's chest protector—a vest, stuffed with cork strips, that he and his wife cobbled together in their kitchen. In the broken-fingers era before catcher's mitts, he was worried about fans "roasting him for being chicken-hearted," and only wore the vest under his uniform.

The year before Bennett joined the Detroiters, he took his position behind the dish for his team, the Worcester Ruby Legs. With Lee Richmond, the game's first dominant lefty, up on the bump, Bennett became the first major leaguer to catch a perfect game. Richmond said of all the catchers he threw to, "My favorite was Charlie Bennett, the best backstop that ever lived in the world. He went after everything, he knew no fear, he kept his pitcher from going into the air."

In 1894, Bennett caught a southbound train with a teammate, the Hall of Fame curveballer John Clarkson. They were headed down to Kansas to do a little hunting and fishing. Bennett never made it to his bass lake. Trying to reboard after a quick stop, he slipped and fell on the wet train platform at precisely the wrong time. He ended the trip—and his baseball career—facing a double amputation.

Bennett Park begot Navin Field, and Navin Field begot Briggs Stadium, and finally, in 1961, new owner John Fetzer took charge and renamed the place Tiger Stadium. It was 340 feet to left, 325 to right, and 440 to straight-way center. Not too big, not too small. A perfectly perfect ballyard redolent with history and the comingled smells of green grass, stale beer, and popcorn.

Our seats were in the lower deck, close in by third base and beside one of the stately blue support columns holding up the upper deck. Because they obstructed views and were considered eyesores rather than character-enhancing throwbacks, these very columns would doom this ballpark in the eyes of the soulless jerks who think baseball is somehow better in cookie-cutter stadiums named after a mortgage company rather than a heroic catcher who sported a dashing handlebar mustache and broke every finger on both hands before his career ended.

I took it all in, nine innings worth of baseball's comforting flow. I pleaded with my old man to stay until the stands were empty and the people were all gone, hoping the lights wouldn't dim and we'd never have to leave.

——

According to my buddy Foghorn, we got turned around somehow and drove into the Deschutes the wrong damn way. I didn't mind. I didn't think there was a "wrong way" to get to a river. The road was green and twisting, and I was perfectly content staring out the truck's window, watching for coyotes, deer, and red-tailed hawks.

Foghorn and I floated through the great canyon the next day, drifting, spinning, and bouncing in the current. Reduced. Immense. The noises of water and wildlife scattering to nothing, joining the ever-shifting sagebrush wind. Only able to mouth the most obvious words—*lotta water . . . awful pretty . . . nice clouds.*

The river canyons of the American West cradle enormity with an ease that's nothing less than astounding. They contain deep, cold miracles—trout and steelhead. Birds parade, high and low. The winds are rubbed with sage. The water is a conversation. It is everything all at once.

The writer David James Duncan describes the essence of wonder as "unknowing experienced as pleasure." That is a river canyon. Wonder unto itself. Wonder, and the mere thought of it—a wonder compounded. Wonder as the lifeblood of that perfect place every angler creates within the heart.

With a dumb little flip—just getting the line out—I caught a fish on my very first cast. A nickel-bright 12'er decided he had to eat that fly. I obliged but knew, in my suspicious angler bones, that I was cursed. I didn't fool another trout for the next two hours.

Later, we stood along a bank broken by basalt rocks and sandbars, the flow punctuated by small, couch-sized islands. Bugs began coming on stronger every moment, popping as they broke the surface. It was a classic, early-season Western assortment: BWOs, March browns, and mahoganies. I grabbed a rod with a grind 'em out combo: size-16 gray parachute Adams and a tiny Quigley emerger. These are generally workmanlike, all-purpose flies, but at the right moment can also be precise, trout-catching machines. It was that moment. It was go time: "Get in the boat, Foghorn!"

We floated two hundred yards to the middle of a greasy, boulder-filled run. "You want up or down?" I asked. Foghorn said he'd be fine right here, next to the boat. I trudged upstream as quickly as the current would allow. Up was what I wanted. I thanked the trout gods. *Up! Yes! That's where the trout were. Why did Foghorn stay put? Who cares. I don't have time to unriddle his bad decisions. Cast. Okay. There it is. No. Cast. No. Yes. Where? Splash! Strike! On!* As they say in the big leagues, there are no ugly hits.

I roped the next two via a combination of trout ESP and intuitive guessing, and made solid contact on the rest. More than one, not quite ten. No huge ones, but no dinks either. Still, strong work on a solid hatch, and I didn't even have to move my feet. The fish ranged from twelve to fifteen inches; some were shiny, some soot covered. "Them's the spawners," said Foghorn. An osprey settled in up on the canyon rim, our only spectator, way up in the cheap seats.

That night we shared a boozy campfire. Two grown men, both suddenly snake experts who'd battled the largest serpents in the Lower 48, defied death, and lived to tell the tales.

"When I was a kid, I found a baby rattler swimming around in my bowl of Cheerios. Didn't faze me. Had a second bowl, as a matter of fact. I ain't scared of no Deschutes rattler, that's for sure."

"Pffft. That's nothin'. When I was twelve, I played little league using a catcher's mitt I stitched together from a six-foot Western diamondback. Hit .387; 17 home runs; 48 RBIs. Threw out every runner dumb enough to try to steal on me. You can look it up."

I started talking about old Charlie Bennett's broken fingers and how, during the off-season, he loved to blow snakes to kingdom come on hunting trips. About old Bennett Park, which became Navin Field which became Briggs which became the wonder of the old Tiger Stadium.

Can you picture it—the Deschutes River Canyon as old Tiger Stadium? Baseball in a box canyon. "Imagine these basalt towers," I said, "supporting that sainted old ballyard. This canyon is our ballyard. To left. To right. To straightaway center. It's perfect." Suddenly, mid-sentence, I was shushed quick and firm.

Listen.

We sat by the snapping fire and heard that basalt come smashing down the immense canyon walls. No, definitely not a train. Certainly not thunder. Rocks. Boulders. Hundreds of them. It was booming, crackling, and splintering. Across the canyon, the rockslide went on-off-on-again for ten minutes. We were silent, alert, the hairs on our arms prickled.

Then it was over. It almost didn't need to be whispered: How great would it be if these rockslides trapped us in here with the lights switched off, all the people gone? We'd never have to leave.

The Post-Capital Wilderness

In a parking lot in Gardiner, Montana, it's still possible to poach Wi-Fi from an unwitting motel along the tiny town's main drag. On Friday mornings, during the trout season's most likely hatches, you can see them there, idling in trucks with plates from Washington, Oregon, Minnesota, and Utah, conducting the bureaucratic whatevers that must be attended to before the ledger closes on the workweek. Men and women in waders squint and tap at keyboards and tablets, filing sales reports, fudging audits, checking in at the office, and thanking the fly fishing gods for inventing this thing called remote work. Me? I was just slack. An aromatic fishing bum filing another unemployment claim and feeling pretty damn clever about it.

From behind the wheel of my beater truck, I quickly sent out the three mandated résumés to jobs I knew I'd never get (investigative reporter, *New York Times*; managing editor, *Advances in Surgical Technique and Practice*; and Paris correspondent, *Glamour Magazine*) and clicked over to the state's rickety website for my weekly online Washington State unemployment-insurance verification exercise. It was a simple process. I'd been unemployed for so long that I knew the questions by heart, but every week, I still had to drive from my campsite somewhere in Yellowstone National Park and sing for my supper.

Question: Were you able and willing to work?
This first question is the toughest. It's loaded with ambiguity. Sure, I was sorta able and kinda willing, I guess. I mean, the fishing is pretty hot right now, and Yellowstone sure is pretty this time of year, and to tell you the

honest-to-god truth, I really don't miss those spreadsheets. So, I'd say I'm able but maybe not so willing. If forced or otherwise compelled, I guess I'd have to show up, but other than something really dramatic . . .

Answer: YES.

Question: Did you accept any money as severance pay or in lieu of vacation days?

No money changed hands. Those bloodsuckers at my previous place of employment were way too cheap to offer any severance pay, and I'd burned through all my vacation days fishing. I mean, that's probably why I'm unemployed right now.

Answer: NO.

Question: Did you fail to go to any scheduled job interviews?

Here's a tip, if you don't schedule a job interview or only apply to jobs you are guaranteed not to get, you won't fail to attend any scheduled job interviews. It's simple math.

Answer: NO.

Question: Did you serve on a jury?

Reckoning that the unrelenting judgment and heckling of fishing buddies does not constitute a jury in the strict civil/legal sense, I can answer honestly.

Answer: NO.

Question: Did you serve in the military?

Army of trout. Heh. Brave lads in Capilene underpants and Copenhagen-stained puffy coats bearing the misery of bean-and-cheese burrito rations, cheap beer, and half-inflated Therm-a-Rest sleeping pads every night. Not to mention the elevation headaches, blistery agony, shoulders wrecked from shotgun casts, swarms of insurgent flies, and propane cylinders tossed into the fire ring. It's hell out there, Sarge.

Answer: NO.

Question: Did you work in self-employment?

I keep telling myself this ain't work, but if I put in this much effort sitting in the cube, I'd make junior assistant deputy shift manager in no time.

Answer: NO.

After a few more button pushes, I hammer "submit" and send the form back to Olympia. The truck starts, and I drive through the north entrance and back into Yellowstone National Park. If you play it cool, you can sneak in the Mammoth Hot Springs Hotel's side entrance, grab a nice, free hot shower, and return to the ol' fishing grind before noon.

4

THE TRUE NAMES

Before mingling with the Pecos River and the Rio Grande to bolster the Amistad Reservoir, the Devils River is the most remote and pristine waterway in Texas. Getting there requires a treacherous, high-clearance, 4x4 creep through some of the most hardscrabble places in the Southwest. And this week, as the guy selling me a bottle of tequila in the dusty village of Sonora puts it, "It's gonna be hot as two rats humping in a wool sock."

Even if you can get *to* the Devils River, five hours southwest of Austin, getting *on* it is another matter entirely. Access is severely limited, and permits to float are a tough ticket. Most of the river is locked up by sprawling ranches. But if there are ranches, where are the cows? Other than barbed wire, punishing scrub, rocks, and the tenacious beasts who call the place home—turkeys, lizards, jackrabbits, vultures, and those lovable vectors of leprosy and other horrible diseases, armadillos—there's not a lot out here. You'd think a cow would sizzle like a hamburger on this griddle. But then, in the middle of nowhere—and I mean *nowhere*—you finally spot the river bottom and descend into the canyon. Everything changes.

Springs finger down the ravine. Green shoots sprout and hold tight. There are live oak and pecan trees. The whiff of herbaceous things—mint, pine, sage—mixes with the smells of hot mud and cool water. Finally.

When the idea of a massive, 8,700-acre Texas ranch with what seems like a mile of waterfront is suggested, you expect something like a villa—a low-slung ranch house with imported tiles, wrought iron, and large, expensive landscape paintings. Not here. The lodgings at the Sycamore Canyon Ranch are nothing more than a well-worn, 1960s-era bunkhouse with a kitchen, bathroom, and a delightful screened-in porch, all hidden in a shady copse of trees just a short path from a wide spot in the river.

The ranch lies at the juncture of the Tamaulipan, Balconian, and Chihuahuan desert ecosystems, anchoring diverse bioregions and habitats that can shapeshift from one canyon to the next. Compared to the desert surrounding it, the riparian band embracing the water is an oasis. Shade and access to cool, flowing water bestows home and shelter to gentler creatures—white-tailed deer, Rio Grande turkey, javelina, quail and doves, waterfowl, and, of course, bass—big, voracious bass.

The ranch hideout is perfect at dusk, with frogs barking, a sweet breeze, and a can of sweating beer on a creaky picnic table loaded with dominos. After the sun surrenders the day, I walk down to the sandy beach to gape at the stars, trying to smell the bass in the flow. Trying to feel them.

Humans have been stargazing from spots like this on the Devils River for eons. Though its most robust civilization probably established a foothold here twelve thousand years ago, it feels like they were just here. They left signs everywhere. This area holds a remarkable trove of Paleo-Indian history—artifacts, tools, petroglyphs, and pictographs. It's a breathtaking moment when Kevin Stubbs, the ranch manager and owner of Expedition Outfitters—and a font of incredible facts—bends down to pick up a rock. But this is not a rock. "See it?" he says. "This did not happen by accident."

The flint fills his fist, but it's meticulously worked, revealing a surprising edge. This is a stone tool—and it's just lying there by the side of a dusty path. I am staring at a relic in the wild. The last person to touch this was the artisan who transformed it from a wedge of flint into an ergonomic, hide-scraping, fish-scaling multi-tool. I was expecting a fishing trip, but I wasn't expecting it to be held at an outdoor natural-history museum.

The ranch's bunkhouse is full. There's a team of marketers from a high-end cooler company "supervising" the shooting of a short promo stoke film. There is the film crew from Austin. There are the two stars—a local fly fishing guide and a pro bass angler from California. Then there's me. What am I doing here? I'm not sure. Nobody is. Cooler companies, it seems, have generous promotional budgets. Budgets indulgent enough to hire a fly fishing writer who may or may not be able to scratch out a few words documenting the place. I'm not writing a script. I'm not working on the film. I don't have an assignment. I'm just . . . here. One thing is certain: the film crew is damn sure my mug is getting nowhere near the production. I'm on my own in the Devils River canyon.

The fly fishing guide is Alvin Dedeaux from Austin. Alvin runs All Water Guides, and I like him the moment I meet him. He tells great stories, laughs easily, and seems free and happy. We talk about the ridiculous and legendary-but-unknown punk bands we played in, shows we saw in basements, squats, and clubs, the mutual pals, and the good old days we both experienced but somehow never shared.

The bass pro introduces himself. "I'm a bass nerd," he says and hands me a business card. It reads Miles "Sonar" Burghoff. "Why do they call you Sonar?" I ask.

"It's my dad," he says. "He was known as Radar. Radar O'Reilly. From the TV show M*A*S*H."

"No," I say.

"Yep," he says.

I really like Sonar, too. He is a huge guy with a sweet smile and soft eyes. He's calm and patient when I ask him dumb questions about being a bass pro. On our first morning, I walk out into a shaded clearing to look for more stone tools. Sonar has set up an aluminum cup in a clearing. He's tossing a swim bait at it with a sly, little underhanded flip from twenty-five feet away. He clangs the lure against the cup nearly every shot. Every few casts, it even goes in. It's impressive. "Flippin' and pitchin', man," he says. "It's what we do."

Alvin wanders over and starts flicking that swim bait at the cup. He's good, too—nailing cast after cast. "It's tough to be a purist as a Texas fly fishing guide," he says with a wink. "We have ten miles of trout water on the Guadalupe River. On the other hand, we have several hundred miles of bass water." I cheer for them both and hope nobody asks me to flip and pitch.

Alvin picks up a fly rod and starts casting at the cup. Sonar casts the fly. They are both ridiculously accurate. "I know for a fact," says Sonar, "that if I had a fly rod on my boat I coulda won two separate tournaments—the bass were being ultra-selective, and I could have caught them on a fly." Alvin nods. If there is any fly-versus-gear enmity between these two anglers, I cannot sense it. Game respects game.

The film crew is up and everywhere, drinking coffee and assembling gear. I decide to hike far downstream to avoid spoiling any water for the shoot. I'm relieved I'm not shooting the film, because shooting films sucks. I've done it. It's tedium and not much fishing. It's fussy. It's multiple takes. It's stunt fish. It's worrying about gear and light and drones. I'd rather fish, thanks.

Kevin, the ranch manager, told me of a cave along the north bank to keep an eye out for. "Full of interesting stuff," he said. It's funny that he expects I'll just stroll into some cave in the Texas desert. Anything could be in there. Hard pass. I start down the path. Now that I know how to identify a piece of worked flint, I begin to spot them regularly. Small chips called chert, larger chunks, pieces that look in-progress but then got rejected and were tossed aside. The number of artifacts is astonishing. They are everywhere.

The Devils is not an ordinary river. It's a time machine. To the north, across a broad limestone bench, is a portal into the life of Paleo-Indian hunter-gatherers—a place where, at the end of the last ice age, men and women stampeded bison off cliffs. Mammoths, saber-tooth cats, camels, and dire wolves patrolled, while families of humans lived in caves and shelters beside this life-giving flow. To my right, the south, is that flow. The light is getting good, and I should probably start fishing.

I catch a fish on my second cast—it's my firmly held belief that it's bad luck to catch a fish so early, but it's worse luck if you think about bad luck too much. This fish is a chunky largemouth, and I grab her by the lip like I think a bass pro would, slip the fly out, and set her free. So far, so good, but I can't help but feel the vibe that hums through this canyon. It is unmistakable, awe-inspiring, and a bit unsettling. I attempt to imagine the civilization that lived here so long ago, for so many hundreds of years. Their faces. How they walked this very path. How their words sounded, their food tasted and what they thought about while staring into this cold, clear water. In the growing heat, I feel a chill. My thoughts drift. Twelve thousand years ago, what did the people who fished here call this river. What is its true name?

Guided by a band of Gueiquesale Indians, Fray Manuel de la Cruz, a lay Spanish Franciscan brother, traveled into this country in 1674 looking to establish a mission. His guides informed him that the river they were descending was called "Decate." Unfortunately, the meaning of this word has been lost to history.

The European colonizers had their own name for the river—the San Pedro—in honor of the apostle Peter. Spain lost their claim to the area in 1821 when the Mexican independence movement forced them to surrender the territory. Mexico's attempt to control the area lasted only until 1836, when the Republic of Texas took over. The Republic lasted for nine years, until the United States annexed it in 1845. Just a few years later, in autumn 1848, the former Texas Ranger Captain Jack Hays was given orders to blaze a new trail from San Antonio to El Paso. Fronting a force of more than seventy men, the expedition made only slow, punishing progress. When they finally reached the river, Hays dismounted, had a look around, and proclaimed, "St. Pete, hell. This is the Devil's River."

I work down the river slowly, casting in all the likely spots. The scene is fabulously lush—almost tropical—and most big blue pools hold bass. In the slower flat sections there are longnose gar—a sixty-million-year-old remnant that somehow found a time lock that staved off evolutionary transformation. The gar ghost after flies, mostly threatening, rarely biting—lizard fish patrolling and protecting territory. I keep moving, hopping across the limestone blocks, mesmerized by the vastness of the scrubland and canyon surrounding this water, wondering if it's time I feel pressing all around me.

After a few hours, the sun lifts over the canyon walls and the heat begins to hammer. Even wet-wading, I'm sweating. That just doesn't happen a lot. A nap sounds good, and after a half-hour on the path back to the bunkhouse, I run into Kevin. We walk down the trail, and he tells me about the famous TV evangelist who would come to the ranch to wander through the shaded rivulets and side channels that cradle the river's main stem. The verdant river bottom, the preacher believed, was just as the Garden of Eden appeared "back in the Bible days." He'd stand in the water for hours at a time, face toward the sun pondering who knows what. He didn't even fish.

Kevin points up the side of the canyon and begins to scramble up. "It's up here," he says. "Follow me. Watch for snakes." There's barely a trail, and everything around it wants to poke flesh, scratch skin, and break bones—one mistake and the vultures will descend.

The cave is a wide-open mouth thirty feet tall by seventy-five feet across. It constricts the farther in you walk. The sharp tang of bat guano is overpowering. Across the opening are piles of rocks layered with fine dust. Kevin points to the roof of the cave. It is blackened by soot from fires lit centuries ago. He points to the boulders and limestone benches along the sides of the entrance. They are rubbed smooth by bodies and hands resting against them. Look closer, he says. I see the straight lines cut into the rock. For sharpening tools, he says. Deep in the cave there are many stone tools, parts of stone tools, and chips from the production of stone tools. The artifacts are strewn everywhere—as if this were both a factory and a living space. I lean against one of the benches in the very same spot the camp fish catchers did eons ago. The view of the river is splendid, even in the brutal, shimmering heat of midday.

The following day, Kevin indulges my questions about the area's natural history and the ancient cultures who lived here. He has a few examples of what can be done when you bang a couple of rocks together. The flint blades are remarkably beautiful and meticulously worked. One artifact, in particular, holds my attention. It is a razor-sharp dagger hewn from zebra flint. It's about six inches long and appears brand new. It glows in the light; it looks dangerous, powerful. "My theory is that this was ceremonial. Maybe it belonged to a shaman," Kevin tells me.

As we chat, the film crew escalates their work pace. They approach "frenzy," packing gear and stuffing kayaks with cases, coolers, and fishing tackle. They are shooting an overnight float-film with Alvin and Sonar and only the most spartan gear, not much food, and no beer. Brutal. I see them off then pack a six-weight, a box of flies, and some water, and head down the trail and into the distant past.

The sun is still hours from its murderous rage, and the fishing is much the same as the day before. Fish here and there, a mix of largemouth and smallies. Devils River largemouth and gar have called this river home forever, but the smallies were introduced in 1957. They are not shy. I fool enough of them to keep spirits high. Exploration. Wonder. A few fish to hand. A bottle of cold water. Combined, they constitute the ingredients for a fine morning.

I've always wondered over the history of rivers—their stories, imagining who fished this spot, who stood on this rock, what were their lives like? How to even begin to think about the massive stretch of time between the present moment and the unfathomable lives of the people who called this canyon home—how do you even get your head around it? I find a deep pool, jump in, and bob around for a while. The water is warm on the surface and cools in its depth. I float on my back, staring up at the canyon walls.

———

Kevin is back at the ranch. It's already nearing one hundred degrees. "Wanna do some exploring?" he asks. Of course I do. "Let's move before it gets too hot to hike," he says.

I throw some water in a pack, hop in Kevin's rig, and think about Alvin and Sonar roasting in their kayaks. It seems cruel. Kevin and I slowly carve down an impossible track until he stops the truck. He steps out, straps on a sidearm, grabs a walking stick, and starts loping up a sketchy trail. I can see the cave opening in the distance, and stumble-bumble behind him as he picks the route.

The mouth of this cave shelter is wide, cool, and inviting. There is shade. It is like a huge front porch, but one that's hidden and easily defended. There are wide sitting rocks and benches, all rubbed remarkably smooth.

The pictographs are everywhere. I can't take my eyes from them, trying to find meaning and decipher what they have to say about the lives these people led. No matter the meaning, the pictographs have accomplished what all art—at its most basic—seeks to communicate: "We were here." As I sit in these people's seats on their front porch, I feel their spirits in my bones.

Just a few steps farther and I stand in a gallery—figures shaded with reds, others the color of a blue-black tattoo. The images are gangly and larger than I anticipated. They are also very, very strange. There are obvious representations of snakes and centipedes, bison and birds, but then there are the humanoid shapes. They seem some peculiar combination of alien and human—figures with horns, tails, and huge, gazing eyes, with odd symbols like lightning bolts surrounding them. Shamans, god talkers, medicine givers, sky swimmers, whisper kings, secret holders.

Another image is composed of four humanoid forms standing together as if dancing. Magic, ritual, river songs.

Creatures float across one of the cave's walls. Could they be rough approximations of fish finning through their river? What did these people call that fish? How did they catch it? What was their name for water? What was their name for this home? What did they call the world around them? Did they have a word for Earth? For themselves?

I can't help but think I'm in the home of a Devils River angler. He would have stood just here, leaning against this cool rock, looking out at the river, wondering if the fish would be biting tomorrow.

According to the research, the hunter-gatherer Paleo-Indians who lived here nine thousand years ago were much shorter than today's humans—5'3" to 5'6" on average. They ate a steady diet of prickly pear, agave, sotol, yucca, birds, and fish. In this early post-glacial period, the area was much wetter than it is now and likely held more game. They hunted using stone points lashed to spears and aided by an atlatl, a shaped stick that assisted the throwing of weapons. They wove with the local grasses, making sandals and clothes. They kept dogs around. They were alert for short-faced cave bears. They went fishing and napped in the shade. "These people were well organized," Kevin tells me. "They had enough time on their hands that they could produce art. That's huge. That means they had abundance. They had everything they needed. These were privileged spots." As we speak, we seem to both whisper as if we were in a church, a graveyard, a sacred spot—all of them.

On our final morning, we tow a raft to a slow, spring-fed, lakelike pool upstream of the ranch. As we float, Kevin points out some underwater structure along the bank—the perfect place for bass to hang out. I start lobbing casts. There are big fish here, and I miss more than I catch. I'm distracted, looking up at the canyon walls hissing in the heat. They were up there, in the caves and shelters. They were down here on this water. They still are.

RIVER SONG

That's Entertainment

"And angle on, and beg to have
A quiet passage to a welcome grave."
—SIR IZAAK WALTON

"Nothing flatters us so much as an obsession with death; the obsession, not death."
—E. M. CIORAN

Slough Creek, the second and third meadows. The world's finest stretch. Beautiful water. Best-looking cutts. Excellent numbers. Wildlife. Weather. Adventure. And after that first forty-five minutes—all uphill—it's easy, rolling terrain to the water. A leisurely amble through the woods. That's what I told the rasping coffin-dodger with a red putty nose, wolf eyes, and puffy, spider-webbed cheeks.

How long? he asked. How far up?

Only two hours, but like I said, the only lung-buster is that first forty-five minutes.

Steep?

Fuck and yes.

The poor old guy looked crestfallen and turned back to the parking lot. He hadn't planned for this. Mortality laughing in your face is a real, gut-chewing disappointment. But, still, the choice was his to make.

You hear it all the time: "I'd love to kick it doing what I love. I want to die on the river. We all gotta go sometimes—and man, what a way to go."

This is romantic talk, but how bad could it be?

To get to the finest stretch in the world, one should be willing to risk it all—to overexert calcified capillaries, rupture an aneurysm, and have spurts of blood saturate the brain. The central nervous system is extinguished before the heart knows it's even in trouble.

To have a pulmonary artery snap off from your heart, gushing blood all over your insides like a garden hose turned on high for a midsummer lawn dance. You gasp and wheeze for forty-five minutes, slowly drowning from the inside out, unable to move, knowing no help is coming.

To have a griz rip the back of your skull off because you wandered between her and her two three-hundred-pound cubs, who, by the way, are perfectly capable of defending themselves. You tumble down a slight slope. The shredded basilar and carotid arteries at the base of your brain fertilize the dirt with a warm hemorrhage spring. Once the adrenalin wears off and your blood pressure begins to free-fall, everything goes quiet and the dirt nap commences. The ravens appear within minutes and begin their work.

To miss a handhold and slip while navigating a rocky descent. The fall breaks a hip and you lie immobile for hours, slipping in and out of shock as the cold of night stiffens every bone and freezes every joint in your body. An hour before the sun finally comes up, you drift into a big, comfy, hypothermic sleep. Forever.

Tying on a fly streamside, you notice that your eyesight is a bit blurrier than usual. These damn, tiny flies, you think. Drawing breath, you look up and lose equilibrium. The horizon tilts and you stumble, attempting to keep balance, but every muscle on the left side of your body has stopped working due to the ischemic stroke depriving your brain of oxygen. You tumble into a deep pool, completely paralyzed, as your lungs fill with the hallowed water from the world's finest stretch.

That's the dream, at least. Good luck out there.

5

SIR LONGBALLS

I couldn't see. A half-dozen headlamps were blinding me. They were right in my face.

"Step back, dudes. I need to get a better angle." Murphy shouldered through the crowd. He was holding a beer in one hand and a couple dental tools—that tiny, round mirror thing and the lethal, two-headed probe—in the other.

I was lying on a picnic table with my mouth open and a bottle of whisky by my head. "I finally gotcha where I want ya, old man," he said. Someone in the peanut gallery hooted about a pretty mouth, that I should never kiss my mother with that thing, something, something . . . blowjob. Everyone was having a great time. Everyone but me.

Lower left 19, a molar, was broken—damaged beyond repair. The gums around the tooth were swollen and hurt like hell. It was kind of loose. It was sensitive to hot and cold. It got angry when I chewed on that side of my mouth, and when my tongue ran exploratory missions to check in on it, there would be electric, stabbing pain.

The tooth really throbbed, but I didn't think it was an emergency. I was used to it. My teeth have been a mess for a decade. In fact, for the last couple of years, Murphy has faithfully asked about what he calls my "poop tooth"—good ol' lower left 19. I'd shrug and say, "Eh . . . it's okay." Truth is, it wasn't okay.

My first excuse is that I am spooked by dentists. The thought terrifies. I get woozy thinking about the bleak white smell of a dentist's office. The metallic drill squeal sparks shiver spasms. I'd rather just stay away. Like lots of men neglecting primary health care, I hoped the thumping pain, the inability to chew, the jolting reaction to stimuli, would just fix themselves—that they would magically vanish as quickly as they'd appeared. I was wrong. Those miracles never happen. God never answers those prayers. I'll admit to being in denial and falling for the tough-guy/pain-don't-hurt narrative, but still, the poop tooth just creeped into my life. I didn't go looking for this trouble, that's for sure; it just snuck up on me.

My second excuse is the system—late-stage capitalism. Since giving up on my corporate nine-to-fiver, I'd been without dental insurance. Hell, I'd been without any insurance whatsoever and in a campsite beside Rock Creek, Montana, the peril of my situation came into sharp focus. One slipup while wading this river—a broken fibula or tibia, a cracked patella, a distal radius fracture, or even something simple, like a full-priced tooth extraction—could plunge me into years of debt. So, the excuses I told myself—daily—about why I was living with a decaying hunk of calcium barely covering a jangly tangle of raw nerve endings in my mouth distilled into two regrettable facts: I was too scared and too broke.

Something else was bugging me. I hated to think this dental setback was because of the onset of old age. I mean, anyone can have a broken tooth—or a mouth full of shitty teeth. Joe Strummer, Shane McGowan, and George Washington had less-than-perfect clackers, and the same still goes for Madonna and Steve Buscemi. But still, I couldn't shake the feeling that this mouth pain signaled my inevitable, age-related decline. I could sense it—especially on the river.

Wading Rock Creek is tough no matter how old you are. It's one of those rivers that's always just a bit faster and a bit deeper than you think, and whose riverbed cobbles epitomize the term "greased bowling balls." Still, I once took pride in my wading skills. I played ultimate frisbee and hockey my whole life. I raced mountain bikes. I consider myself a very groovy dancer.

Strong legs and good balance are the solid parts of my game. But these days, I never leave trout camp without a wading staff. Every year, I make sure I have fresh studs in my boots. I wade slowly, carefully. I tell myself that a more careful pace will scare fewer fish—that part may even be true. But the fact is, at my age, I just can't afford a fall and a broken bone. At my age, I have enough problems to deal with. At my age . . . At my age.

"All right, you ready for this?" Murphy asked. I nodded. It was time for the main event. "Okay, open up, honey." My fishing buddies hooted. I looked around, trying to find an exit route, but couldn't see anything thanks to those headlamps shining in my eyes.

"Wait a sec . . . just wait a sec . . . I need to get a breath. Just gimme a minute."

Everyone hooted and booed. Called me names. Pushed the whisky bottle in front of me, like they were doing me a favor—a last gulp for the dead man walking, straggling up to the gallows.

I'm not sure I really trusted Murphy as a dentist. I wasn't even sure he *was* a dentist. I'd never seen him in scrubs and a white coat. He didn't really strike me as professional. I'd only encountered him once a year at this late-season fish camp where he'd sit around drinking beer and smoking weed like any other fishing degenerate with a weeklong hall pass. I'd never even heard him talk about his day job. The only time he mentioned his formal training was when he recounted how he'd get jacked up on speed in dental school to stay up all night cramming for finals. When I heard the story, I thought, "Man, that's commitment." I never imagined he'd be poking around in my mouth with sharp tools and serious intent.

As it turned out, a toothache was the least of my problems. I had troubles in the basement, too—troubles I couldn't conceive of confessing to my fish-camp crew. They had begun a couple years earlier when, at the age of fifty, my nuts began to grow. One day, I was just a guy with what I considered a generous set. The next, I could barely fit into blue jeans, and all my pals were calling me Sir Longballs. It was funny for five minutes, but then I really began to worry.

What could it be? Probably cancer. What were the remedies? Surgery? Chemo? Radiation? No matter what, it was certainly not going to be pleasant. And what about the prognosis? Like everyone else who has ever faced their mortality, I thought it was too early for me. And even if I did heroically manage to pull through, what would my quality of life be? Incontinence? No more sex? Every option was awful. I hated thinking about it, but I couldn't stop myself. I signed up for Obamacare. No dental coverage, but the tooth paled in comparison to the situation with my testicles.

I'm terrified of doctors, too—of the cost, of the poking, of what they might find—all of it. The clinic blares harsh fluorescent lights, grimy white paint, colorless carpets, the smell of disinfectant. The day I went in, I immediately wanted to bolt, run back to my house, and google a folk remedy. Instead, a nurse stepped from behind a closed door and mispronounced my name. I felt myself rise and walk toward her.

My heart was thumping as the nurse began asking me the routine questions. She strapped the cuff to my arm and pumped up the sphygmomanometer. "It's a bit above normal," she said.

"Well, I'm really, really anxious," I said.

"I get it. We see it all the time. Has it been a while since you've seen a doctor?"

She was good. She pegged me immediately.

"Guilty as charged," I said. "Sorry."

"So, what brings you in to see the doctor today?"

I was dreading everything about this visit, but I'd envisioned this part in my mind many times—the part where I'd have to talk to a complete stranger about my private parts. I'd been dealing with this for how long now? A year? Eighteen months? I couldn't even put a timestamp on it. I couldn't think back. All I could grasp was the fear of now and the desire for this moment to be over.

I reminded myself to be as clinical as possible with the nurse. I wanted to use all the correct medical terms and not resort to crude or clever synonyms for my junk.

"Well . . . you see . . . there's something that's not quite right with my testicles. . . . "

The nurse nodded and wrote everything down. I averted my gaze as I described my symptoms. My voice was a little shaky. At the end, I said what I was thinking out loud. I just blurted it out: "I'm scared."

"The doctor will be right in," she said.

<hr>

"C'mon . . . let's get back to the poop tooth, dude," Murphy said. "I promise you—as your friend and as a doctor—I will not hurt you. Remember, I took an oath."

"Were you stoned for that, too?"

"Seriously, if you have an abscess, you want to know. Like I said, I promise I won't hurt you and I won't do anything without asking you first. Okay? Trust me."

"Famous last words."

Foghorn brought over one of those fully reclining camp chairs from the firepit. "Here ya go, buddy," he said. "Nice and comfy."

I edged for the chair. My oldest friends began chanting, "POOP TOOTH! POOP TOOTH! POOP TOOTH!"

<hr>

For many of us, just the thought of a doctor's visit—a regular, standard-operating-procedure checkup—is an anxiety-provoking way to ruin the week leading up to the appointment. When you are sure that the visit will involve a frank discussion of your reproductive organs and the act of pulling down your pants, that anxiety turns to pure, 100-proof dread. True to form, I wasn't at my best leading up to the appointment. Not only was the embarrassment of the visit bumming me out, but lurking behind that bogeyman was the real fear—the thought of what might come out of the doctor's mouth regarding my condition.

He breezed into the examining room with that unbothered combination of busy and friendly so many doctors have perfected. We shook hands, and he picked up the tablet in the room and began reading about me as I stood there dumbly, waiting for him to ask me a question or to issue a command—stick out your tongue, turn your head and cough, drop your trousers.

"So," he said, "What's up? What's going on with you? How can I help?"

"Well," I said, "I'm just going to be direct because I can't think of any other way to say it: My testicles are huge, doc. I think something is really wrong." I exhaled. I felt woozy but better for finally confiding in someone who'd gone to medical school.

"Gotcha. How long have you noticed this problem?"

I began explaining. Telling him the whole story, using only the word *testicles*.

"Well," he said, "a picture's worth a thousand words. Let's take a look."

Is it crazy to admit that I'd picked out my best, newest pair of underpants because I knew this moment was coming? I did. If the doctor noticed, he didn't say anything. Instead, he got to work with the examination. I turned my head and looked away.

"Okay," he said, snapping off his blue latex gloves, "That's it. That's all."

I hiked my pants back up, buttoned my trousers, and exhaled.

"What you have—I'm 99 percent certain—is called a hydrocele. It's not serious. I see them all the time." He explained the condition to me. Typically, the testicles are surrounded by a smooth, protective internal sac. You can't feel it. You don't even know it's there. Its only job is to produce a small amount of lubricating fluid to allow the testes to move freely. If there's any excess fluid in this sheath, it is supposed to drain away via the veins in your scrotum. If that process stops working and the fluid begins to accumulate, that's a hydrocele. The doctor assured me that I would not die, and sent me off with an appointment to see a urologist to take care of the problem.

"That thing is dead," said Murphy, "D-E-A-D dead. That's the deadest tooth I've ever seen. I'm surprised it's still hanging in there." He poked at it with the probe. "It looks like it's a little bit infected, but the nerve is just shot. It's gone. Damn. It'll probably fall out on its own, or if you want, I can pull it out right here. It probably won't even hurt that much."

This bulletin was too much for the crowd. They erupted in wild hoots and started yelling at Murphy—to pull that tooth, pull that tooth! Pull! That! Tooth!

"Hold on a minute, man," I said. "That's demented. Are you seriously telling me you want to pull a tooth out of my skull in the Bitterroot Flat Campground in the middle of nowhere? What are you going to use, 20-pound test and a pair of fishing pliers? How am I supposed to fish tomorrow with a molar-sized hole in my head?"

I didn't have testicular cancer. I wasn't scheduled to die (yet). I felt great, even though I was pulling open the door to an office with the word "Urologist" screen-printed on it. I did the usual stuff—height, weight, blood pressure—and, within a few moments, the urologist appeared. He was an older guy. I imagined how many pairs of balls he'd seen in his career—thousands, I'm sure. It wasn't that I thought seeing so many people's privates was odd or strange or anything. It's just that, well . . . that's a lot of testicles and a lot of variety.

I couldn't help but recall a Saturday-afternoon assignment I'd volunteered for as a reporter in Boise, Idaho. The idea behind a "Testicle Festival" was to herd hundreds of folks into the local rodeo grounds, lubricate 'em with beer, spray 'em with country music, and then feed 'em what they called "Rocky

Mountain oysters," "swinging beef," "sack lunch," "tendergroin," or any of a dozen other nicknames for breaded and deep-fried bull testes.

On the day of the festival, I arrived at the fairgrounds before the crowds. I watched a small assembly line of Stetson-wearing men and women slice open the membrane surrounding nut meat and remove the potato-sized testicles. They discarded the membrane and sliced the "bull's eggs" into coins about ¼-inch thick. Those membranes—that was my problem right there. For both the bulls and me, the membranes—and what they held—had led to nothing but trouble.

The "cowboy canapés" were seasoned, breaded, dunked into hot oil, and sold to patrons for ten bucks a portion. The nutsteaks were a hit. Everyone was laughing, teasing one another, egging each other on. They made faces when they ate them, but they couldn't get enough. They'd say, "Ya know, they're not too bad!" and slap each other on the back.

I thought the Rocky Mountain oysters were unremarkable. They didn't taste like anything but the mayo/ketchup dipping sauce and the old fryer grease. But it was the texture that got me. They were like a cross between a boiled hot dog and a sautéed sponge. *Bleh.*

"Well," said the urologist, "I can tell you that's definitely a hydrocele—and it's a doozy, my friend. A world-class specimen. Let's get this taken care of."

———

"Look," Murphy said, "this thing is not going to get better on its own. The nerves are gone. The tooth is rotten. It ain't comin' back." Everyone leaned in, listening intently, like young dental students at their first tooth-pulling lesson. And after what was pretty much a perfect day of fall fishing on Rock Creek, this was the finest après angling entertainment ever—for everyone but me.

"Here are your options, as far as I see them," said the alleged dentist. "Number one: You can leave it in there. It will continue to hurt. The infection could get worse, and you could be in a lot more pain. Number two: you could go back into Missoula, find a dentist who might see you, and have him pull it. Or, number three: I could yank it right here in about five minutes." The crowd—most still in their waders—hooted, as before, "Pull that tooth! Pull that tooth!"

The procedure to treat a hydrocele is simple. A local anesthetic is injected into the scrotum, and, after everything is good and numb, a syringe is inserted to drain the accumulated fluid. Sounds simple. It should be easy. Foolproof. A slam dunk.

It didn't take. After a few weeks, the hydrocele had returned as plump, bull-like, and robust as ever. I went in again for another procedure. "It'll work this time. I'm almost sure of it," said the doc. "I've done thousands of these."

"What if it doesn't?"

"Then we go to plan B."

After a month, the hydrocele returned. I had to face whatever Plan B had in store for me.

Plan B, the doctor said, was the knife. I had no choice. I was scheduled for surgery—the dreaded hydrocelectomy, a.k.a. the "Western Snip, Stitch, and Tug" repair. It sounds like instructions on how to tie a salmon fly. The procedure has an excellent success rate and promises reduced pain, inflammation, infection, and discomfort for the patient.

Here's how it's done: A two- to three-centimeter incision is made into the scrotum over the spermatic cord. The cord is lifted through the wound and gentle pressure on the scrotum is used to manipulate the hydrocele sac so that it's visible in the incision. The sac is punctured, and the hydrocele fluid is drained. The sac is turned outward, bringing the free edges behind the spermatic cord and testes. These edges are then fixed in place with a single figure-of-eight suture. Gentle traction on the scrotum pulls the testes back into position. To finish, tissue and skin are closed via absorbable sutures. In my case, a small tube was inserted into the incision to continue draining the area after the surgery.

This is not a good time.

I crawled up from under the anesthetic dazed, confused, and in exquisite pain. The fluorescent lights were harsh, the smells were acrid and sharp, there were strangers everywhere, and my groin was packed and wrapped like a pharoah from Egypt's great tombs.

The recovery was excruciating, awkward, and honestly really scary. Fortunately, my partner was around to lighten my mood with her silly testicular puns, gentle teasing and encouragement. In about a week or so, I was back on my feet, walking around in pants that fit a bit more comfortably. I was grateful to be healthy again.

But after a couple of months, I noticed something again wasn't quite right. The cursed hydrocele was back—again. It was unthinkable. My doctor said it was against all odds. I was scheduled for another surgery. It was fall. In my neighborhood, off the beaches of Puget Sound, salmon were running. I couldn't fish. I couldn't even think about the future.

"What about aftercare," I pleaded to Murphy. "What happens after you pull that tooth? Do I just swish my mouth out with some Maker's Mark, hop on my horse, and ride off into the sunset? What the fuck, dude? What about an infection? What about dry socket? I've heard of that, and it really doesn't sound cool!"

"Well, you're right," he said. "You don't want dry socket. But we can pack some gauze into the hole, and you should be fine. From the looks of that sucker, it probably won't even bleed that much."

"Look," I said, "we've only got four or five more days here. I'll be fine after a couple beers, okay? I don't feel like bleeding out on the banks of Rock Creek."

"What are you so afraid of? If you can give us one good reason why we shouldn't pull that tooth right here, right now, I'll leave you alone."

It was the decisive moment.

The second time under the knife was even worse than the first. Everything hurt more. The recovery was more painful and took longer. My mood was crabbier. But slowly, my wounds healed and my attitude improved, just in time for the annual trip to Rock Creek with the fellas.

One of the traditions on this trip is that everyone has a night when they are responsible for making dinner for the rest of the crew. It's a serious task, and everyone brings their A game. The feasting is epic. We've had everything from ribeye to walleye fry-ups, all manner of T-bones, tenderloins, birria tacos, venison chili, and smoked BBQ brisket. It's awesome.

My plan was simple: balls. I'd start by unraveling the hydrocele story while I prepped the kitchen and made cocktails for the gang. I'd cook while I told the story—the needles, the sutures, the operation, every bloody detail. Then I'd fire up the appetizer. Set up a sauté pan with some olive oil on medium heat. I'd open the vac-sealed pouch and slide the already-breaded portions into the oil. Just as my tale reached a crescendo, they'd be done: a steaming-hot plate of Rocky Mountain oysters with authentic dipping sauce. Bon appétit!

"All right. Fuck it. Let's do it."

Murphy pumped his fist and said, "Yes!" The crowd cheered and got their cameras ready. He dug through the small Dopp kit that had produced the probe and mirror. "I always carry a few tools with me," he said. "In case of . . . well, this." He held up a medieval-looking pair of pliers for all to see. "These, gentlemen, are extraction forceps. German made. Stainless steel. Matte finish. Quite ergonomic."

A roll of paper towels had appeared. Some ice was scooped out of the cooler. Murphy was snapping on rubber gloves and unwrapping a roll of gauze.

"Let's do this," he said.

I took a swig of the whisky. I needed it. I made the sign of the cross. I was being dramatic. I reclined into the chair. Everyone pushed closer and clicked their headlamps to blazing. "I forgot I even had this lidocaine in here. You're in luck. Open up," Murphy said. He stuck his finger in my mouth and rubbed it on my gums.

"Yep," I heard him say. "There she blows." He let everyone step up and get a good look. "Okay . . . hold on. I'm gonna count to three."

One . . . the crowd howled the number along with him.

And then he pulled the tooth. He didn't count to three. He yanked it on "one" and the tooth popped out easily. He was right. It was over before it began. It didn't even hurt.

"There it is!" he shouted. Everyone was stunned, then everyone hollered, "Hooray!" Everyone wanted to see it, but no one wanted to hold it. It looked as nasty in my palm as it felt in my mouth. Dirty yellow and mottled brown with jagged roots. "That's it. That's the whole thing—roots and all," he said. "Came out in one piece, too."

I gingerly pushed my tongue over. I tasted blood and probed the hole with my tongue. I spit red. Murphy handed me a wad of gauze. "Here," he said. "Get this in there. Don't fuck with it for awhile."

Everyone was looking at me, but the drama was over. I was fine. I wrapped the poop tooth in a paper towel and put it in my pocket.

I sat back down to catch my breath, glad to be feeling reasonably okay.

Finally, after a round of fresh beers had been cracked, I'd been congratulated for my bravery, Murphy had been praised for his technique, and the whole ordeal retold once or twice, someone finally asked, "Whose turn is it to cook tonight?"

RIVER SONG

Unknowable

"When you break it down, there is no better way to catch a trout. No other technique even comes close. If there are rising fish and your fly selection is on point, a fly is the best way to catch them. Not a spinning rod, not bait, not nothing. A fly will do the job better than anything."

He ran his fingers through his beard and clinked the ice cubes around the bottom of his bourbon. "But, when it comes to swinging flies for steelhead, it is the absolute least efficient way to catch them. We spend thousands of dollars on the finest boutique gear, but we are entrenched in a paradigm that limits our success. We intentionally make a hard thing harder. Why?"

"Purity," he said. "But not purity in the monastic sense. Purity in a way that distills the connection with a wild fish to its very essence. When that connection is made, we taste what it means to be wild—that cannot be approached, cannot be apprehended by those who have not stepped in the river. It fills us with the unknowable."

"That's the obvious thing," he said, "but not the only thing. On the river, the emptiness fills us. The aloneness fills us. The nothingness fills us, and that, too, is everything. That, too, cannot be faked." He exhaled, put his glass down, and pushed his hands close to the campfire.

6

THE GNARLIES

The Gnarled Islands are a mystery—primordial, raw, hidden. They are difficult to find on a map. Even with GPS coordinates, they appear as tiny, pixilated blobs floating off the northeast coast of Dundas Island, a good twenty-five-minute floatplane trip from Prince Rupert, British Columbia. The area is isolated and pristine. With its desolate loveliness comes a stubborn refusal to reveal any part of itself—its history, its habits, its secrets. The Gnarled Islands have been this way forever.

The Tsimshian, who have populated northern coastal British Columbia since prehistory, made a few forays from their earliest settlements into the Gnarled Islands, but for the most part they stayed close to their longhouse-filled towns. Why risk the long paddle into the turbulent Hecate Strait when food was plentiful at home? The islands were left to themselves, unnamed, unvisited, unmolested.

"We just call 'em the Gnarlies," says Clayton Vanier. Every year, Vanier tows his floating fishing lodge—Haa Nee Naa—into a hidden bay amidst the small cluster of islands. "I don't know how they got the name, 'Gnarled,'" he says, "but I can only assume it's from the gnarly-looking trees on the islands."

Given the lack of hard info about this place, Vanier has named most of the islands himself: Holiday Island, White Island, Kelp Point, The Wall, Two Knobs, J Point, Wolf Island. They stretch in a crescent in front of the soft water where he has anchored his lodge for the season. The island's escarpments are topped with dwarfed and twisted cedars, which have fought the winds for generations. There are small, perfect coves encircled by immense kelp forests. Occasionally, a surprising beach with white sand guarded by ravens or eagles, engaged in a never-ending turf battle for the tallest tree, will appear around a corner.

It's comforting that this place has no known names; that its colonizer identity has been erased and those given to it by the First People are a well-preserved secret. It's better to think of the Gnarled Islands as a place where names don't hold and time isn't measured by a calendar. It is a place where what really matters is the tide, the phase of the moon, and the prevailing winds. Some five miles to the north is the imaginary line that separates the Alaska Panhandle from Canada, but this is still Tsimshian territory and the *laxsgiik* (eagles) don't notice the border, the breaching *gispwudwada* (orca) never stop to ask about names, and the *hawn* (salmon) only follow the maps described by *shga* (herring).

From out of nowhere, the silver salmon arrive angrily, suddenly. Eight or twelve large coho flash in front of our small aluminum boat. They swim in formation and smash into the gigantic herring ball, morphing and shapeshifting below the boat. The salmon are moving incredibly quickly and with a precision I'd never even contemplated. These coho are not really "chrome bright" or "hot." These are wild fish living in the ocean, doing what wild ocean fish do: hunting, killing, flashing from meal to meal in gangs. It is violent, startling.

All around us, squadrons of silvers scream into the bait balls, terrorizing the flashing schools of herring. The ocean surface explodes with salmon battering herring. We lob Clousers tied to full-sinking lines forty or fifty feet into the melee. *Strip. Strip. Strip. Blammo!* No real need for subtlety. Hammer the hook home, hold on, and pray the knots hold and the rods don't shatter. Tied into a fierce, twelve-pound ocean-going coho, knots do fail and rods do explode, but the action is so intense that broken gear is discarded like a blown-up hockey stick. The action is unrelenting, panicked, fraught with excited, stupid mistakes one moment and an ESP-like connection to the silvers the next. The fish are beautiful and terrible. When we catch them, their throats are stuffed with herring and they spit half-digested gobs onto the deck.

The Gnarlies hold us in a lee, protecting us from the wind for an hour, and then the bait goes to wherever the bait goes. The silvers evaporate, and it is over for a few moments. The tide crests and begins to fall. Everyone and everything exhales.

The object is simple. Catch a salmon—a pelagic coho in the salt. It's the odds that are troublesome. Consider the facts: You are throwing a 1.5-inch Clouser into the incomprehensible vastness of the ocean. One fly versus miles and miles of what? Water. Tide. Current. You can't hold tide. You can't put current in a bucket and look at it. You can't think of a number to express how huge the ocean is. Gallons? Gallons mean nothing when you are adrift in a sixteen-foot boat with only an outboard engine separating you from oblivion in a place with no real name.

But odds. The odds of catching a fish by throwing a fly into the ocean— THEY ARE LONG ODDS. Dumb odds. Stupid odds. Vegas would love those odds. And those odds are compounded by the fact that the fly you chuck— if you can execute the cast—will meld with thousands upon thousands of herring, the things you seek to imitate. When you stare into the clear, cold Pacific, it's impossible to count the number of herring in a bait ball. They carpet the bottom of the sea. When they appear on the fish finder, the screen turns black. How many? Ten thousand per bait ball? Ten thousand times ten? The mind boggles. Your fly joins that multitude of panicked, swirling baitfish, and the odds increase like a roulette table set with every color of the spectrum and the numbers 00 to infinity. One in 10,000. One in 50,000. One in 750,000. Imagine any huge number and toss a grain of sand into the desert. Place your money, make your bets, good luck.

But then it happens. You are connected to a fish. It's impossible. So why—how—does one enraged, hungry coho select your fly? How did you beat the odds? What makes *you* so lucky?

Vanier shrugs at the question and checks the GPS. "Hell, I don't really know," he says with a laugh. "I'm thinking they just want the easy meal—the easy target." He points his rod tip into the water at yet another huge school of roiling herring. "See that there—that wounded one?" Immediately my eyes flash to a tiny fish wavering twenty feet below the surface. It's obvious and in plain sight. That tiny bit of living protein is distressed. He swims on his side erratically. His flanks flash in the glinting. Continues Vanier, "Look at him. We both see him clearly, and if we can see that poor bastard from up here, you bet that the coho can see him too."

"You can see that there just aren't that many seals around here," Vanier tells me as we motor around the speck of rock and cedar he's dubbed Wolf Island. "The wolves around the Gnarlies keep the seal population down. We see them up here from time to time, and they swim between the islands. They are really powerful swimmers. They hunt seals that are sleeping on the beach. It's probably pretty easy pickings." He's right, but what the area lacks in seals, it makes up for in eagles, humpbacks, and orcas. The water teems with plankton, and the air has the unmistakably fecund brace of simultaneous growth and decay.

We chug a few minutes from Wolf Island out to J Point and anchor next to an underwater bull-kelp forest to wait for the herring to appear. Without warning, the water ripples with massive explosions, as if bowling balls had begun raining from the sky. "There they are! They're here!" Vanier says, giggling. "Get ready, boys." In a breath, coho are busting the surface, howling topwater to smash herring. We chuck long casts and shout at the fish, "Eat, goddammit, eat!" The fish eat, and again we are hooked up and getting our asses handed to us by wild, desperate animals.

Long odds be damned—if the salmon are there, they are hunting. If your wounded-looking fly is wobbling through their target area, hang on. After six or ten fish to hand, fly fishing perversity kicks in and we attempt to make a hard thing harder. We must double down. I will bet, I smirk at *txaamsm* (raven), that I can catch an ocean-running coho on a bug designed to trick bass on a bathwater-warm farm pond somewhere in the American South.

We want to catch them on top, and the only way to accomplish that is to tie on a popper, aim for roiling water, and start shouting, "Eat goddammit, eat!" The popper skids across the water as a baseball-sized field of bait pops the surface and big coho swirl all over the horizon. If the strikes on the sinking line are violent, the topwater hits are wicked. These are not sippers or gulpers; these hits are thunder. We break two new flyrods in twenty minutes. Flies are demolished. Reels smoke. I worry if I've got enough 15-pound tippet. Haa Nee Naa's head guide, Jason Bower, grins and shakes his head. "Don't worry about a leader, eh," he says, "I usually just use straight 25-pound test."

It is next to impossible to concentrate on a pod of rampaging coho when a gigantic humpback whale is surfacing one hundred yards from your boat. When that whale rolls on her back and starts slapping her fins on the ocean's surface, forget casting. It can be difficult to simply draw breath. And when that massive, ancient mammal swims even closer and launches her body into the air, somehow heaving her tremendous bulk clear of the water and splashing down with a wallop, you must stop and ask, "Did that really happen?" It is nothing less than magnificent. A gift. How many have seen this? How often can you get so close to enormity, to a living, breathing force of nature? Not many, I'd warrant, and not that often. I grip the gunwale, the knuckles on both of my hands white as bone. Three eagles fly overhead, and the whale, now joined by two others, detours into a small cove to bubble-feed on the herring.

"The herring are the life of the ocean," says Bower. "If there are no herring, there is no salmon, no whales . . . none of it." There is plenty of herring this year, and Bower tells us this is the best salmon year in the last six. They are connected. The salmon depend on the herring. "During a good year like this," Bower says, "these coho can put on up to a pound a week. We've counted more than sixty herring stuffed into salmon bellies when we clean them back at the lodge."

Bower is right. The baitfish are everywhere amongst this jumble of islands, current, and tide. If one thing is known about the Gnarlies, it is this: they are a baitfish breeding ground.

It's not just the salmon who are hungry. Herring are feed for everything here. Flocks of gulls patrol between islands, dive-bombing schools. Eagles perch in the tallest trees, awaiting the scraps and the offerings of the low tide. Humpback whales herd herring across the horizon. When the whales surface and exhale, their breath smells of both the sea and the herring—a belch of partially digested fish.

According to archaeological records, Pacific herring, *Clupea pallasii*, have been fished in the northwest Pacific Ocean for more than ten thousand years. In Russia, they were known as "holy bread." In Japan, the Ainu people called them "God fish." Along the northwest coast of North America, they were called the "feed for everything." As fuel and a foundation species for the whole marine food web, herring are crucial for what's known as their ecosystem service: providing food for other aquatic species, indicating water quality and overall ecosystem health, and giving nutritional, social, and cultural benefits to humans. This tiny silvery flash is, to many, the most important fish in the sea.

Historically, Indigenous populations in North America harvested herring up to two months before the fish spawn. Herring could be eaten fresh, smoked, dried, or rendered into oil. The herring eggs that covered the seaweed, eelgrass, and hemlock boughs—these latter carefully placed by gatherers to catch and collect the eggs— are traditional delicacies and are still harvested by Native communities today.

But herring are in trouble. The tipping point traces as far back as the 1870s, when commercial interests seized the herring fishery from Native populations and built a rendering plant in Southeast Alaska. After millennia of sustainable use, the underpinnings of an ecosystem and culture were about to be decimated.

Used for food, the Alaskan harvest in 1878 was 15 tons. By the 1920s, motorized seine boats, new rendering plants, and new markets for bait, fertilizer, and feed sent the herring populations plummeting. In 1937, 125,000 tons of herring were processed in Alaska's reduction plants. By 1939, the population had collapsed, and Alaska prohibited all herring fishing except for bait. The respite didn't last long.

Canadian and American fishing regulations were based on shaky science, had abandoned local and traditional knowledge, and skewed toward promoting extraction at any price—damn the salmon, damn the whales, damn it all. For decades, the senseless, idiotic cycle repeated: herring populations collapsing every few years and in multiple locations, sometimes teetering on the knife-edge of their capacity to rebound.

Unfortunately for the herring, a new market for their sac roe—*kazunoko*—emerged in Japan in the 1970s. Since Japan's own herring stocks had crashed due to overfishing, that harvest zeroed in on North America. Japanese and Russian trawlers did the heavy lifting, and, once again, herring were in grave peril. Processors stripped the fish of the valuable egg sacs while the rest was ground into feed and—to add insult to injury—often pressed into pellets as feed for the ecologically disastrous net-pen, hatchery-salmon farming industry.

In a recent report, the conservation group Pacific Wild called for a closure of the herring kill fishery in British Columbia: "Without immediate, drastic conservation measures, which must include a complete moratorium on the kill fishery—at least until populations have rebounded and science has had a chance to catch up—Pacific herring will remain in peril as will every other species in the marine food chain that relies on herring for its survival."

Numerous Native communities up and down the coast have been asking for the same thing for years. In many cases, Tribes have had little response, though some have sought legal remedy in British Columbia. However, the intermittent closures in British Columbia and Alaska have not stabilized populations, as herring can take a decade to recover.

It's easy to feel the flush of abundance when you're chucking flies into incalculable balls of herring while salmon are eating and, a hundred yards away, whales are breaching. But abundance is a tricky concept, and herring populations are slippery things to contextualize. However, when a scientist tells you industrial herring fishing is like the clear-cutting of the ocean, it brings the problem into sharp focus.

Was that week coho fishing in northern British Columbia an illusion? A look back into the abundant past? A reminder of how herring connect everything? Probably all three. But what is incontrovertible is that overfishing is the root of the herring's troubles—and when herring are in trouble, *everything* is in trouble. The science is clear: most of our exploited herring populations collapsed in the twentieth century, and overfishing is implicated as the most prevalent cause.

On my last afternoon on the Gnarled Islands, my fly snags on some kelp while I'm retrieving line. The kelp is clad in hundreds of pearlescent herring eggs. The eggs are tiny and fragile, less than two millimeters in diameter. During the spawn, a herring may lay more than twenty thousand—but only one out of ten thousand eggs may produce an adult. Long odds.

I scrape the eggs off with my fingers and scoop them into my mouth, holding them on my tongue before popping them between my teeth. They taste like the beginning of everything.

Pressure Drop

It's hard to just sit there—waiting. Nothing to do. Drink some more water. Drink a Kalik, but don't make too much noise rustling around in that cooler. Ponder the fly box and attempt to hide from the determined Bahamian sun. Fret about the wind and the clouds but cheer at the thought of the fried conch with rice and peas that the ladies in the lodge kitchen, fattened by kindness, have in store for dinner. Tend line for Kasper, the fishing bum from Sweden, who won't stop twirling that pink-assed bonefish fly between his fingers. Comment on the wind. Say something to break the silence: "Man, this point sure looks fishy." No one responds. Mutter something else to the guide or to Kasper or to the wind. Try to remember the lyrics to "Pressure Drop" by Toots and the Maytals. The Specials covered that song. Keith Richards had a go. So did The Selecter. The Clash put out a ripping version too. It's the perfect song for a bonefish skiff. The song's writer, Toots Hibbert, said the song was about karma. The lyrics are straightforward. The melody is insanely catchy, and once your brain queues it up, it won't stop playing it: " . . . pressure drop, oh pressure."

Since grabbing the first bone on the first cast of the morning, I view forty-five minutes of Kasper's failures, flubs, screwups, and fumbles as a personal attack—a conspiracy to keep me not fishing while he takes forever on the boat's casting deck. But I shut up about someone else's bad luck. It's bad luck to talk about bad luck. It's even worse luck to take pleasure in someone's bad luck. It's fly fishing karma.

"I don't know how that lead bone didn't eat that fly, man," Kasper says, gesturing toward the flats. He shakes his head and looks at his bare feet. "He was all over it. Why didn't he eat?"

He's not really asking me, but I answer anyway: "Sometimes life ain't fair, dude."

"Yeah," he says. "It almost never is."

"You're breaking my heart back here. Catch a fish, for cripes sake. For both of us."

Mikey Bones, our guide, relights his spliff and I spark a cigarette. Even over the mingling smoke, the stink of desperation is acrid and burning. Mikey is considered one of the finest guides on the planet. Long dreads and a big smile make him instantly recognizable—a friendly face in the fly fishing magazines—but out on the flats, he's all business.

Mikey asks Kasper, "You seen that fish out there comin' strong to the boat?"

"Yeah, I saw it."

"Then why you cast so short?"

Silence. Ears burn. Somewhere a gull cackles. The sun continues to punish. "You can't put the puck in the net if you're gripping the stick too tight," I offer. It's a lame thing to say. I don't even know if Kasper likes hockey.

"Ya get down, now. Ya take a break," Mikey finally tells Kasper.

This is no way for me to take back the casting deck, but Kasper just shrugs, sighs, and reels up. Resigned. A failure.

The sun seems even more intense on deck. The winds never abate. But things are brighter, more in focus. Even the smells—mangroves and mud—wet or baked, soaked or withering, are easier to perceive. The clouds play hide and seek with the sun. I try to remember the names of the clouds. Stratus, cirrus, alto. I think of the word *cumulus* and let it roll around my mouth. It feels cloudlike. I put names to the clouds lining up to cover the sun—Snoop Dogg, Godzilla, Beast Mode, The Cathedral. I congratulate myself for thinking of the cloud word *nimbus* even as that cloud—a huge bird shape about to swallow the sun—is whisked away by the wind.

The light splotches across the flat, and somehow a fish sneaks past our famous guide's famous eyes and glides left to right across the skiff's bow—a mere thirty feet away. The wind has somehow receded into a slight howl.

Even I can see that fish. Even I can make that cast. I put the fly out there before the guide sees the fish and can claim it, but it looks too far to the right. He's never even gonna see it. But no. The bone slows, turns, and starts tracking the fly. Yes. I give a long, slow strip. I can't imagine stripping this fly any slower or any smoother. Long strip. Smooth strip. *Looooong* strip. *Smoooooth* strip.

"Stop stripping. Stop the fly. Cause dem a crash," Mikey whisper-shouts. "Make him bump into it. He gon' take or he gon' turn and run. Right in they face, man."

I stop the fly. One more tiny twitch and he's on. I don't even have time to trout-set. The bone is well hooked and bolts on his first run, speeding off with everywhere and nowhere to go.

That is ridiculous luck for a mediocre angler. I wash the bonefish slime off my hands and shirt, and reach for a victory Kalik. Kasper steps up on the deck whistling "Pressure Drop." He's got the melody right. He's doing a sassy little skank dance. We all join together and shout-sing the chorus to the clouds and the water and the fish.

Things are about to get even better.

7

CUE THE TANGO SCENE

"When in Rome, write shit down."

—AUTHOR UNKNOWN

Unless you live there, Argentina always begins in an airport, somewhere. I start in Seattle—about as far from Argentina as you can get. It's midnight when I settle into the plane for the first flight. I have forgotten my earplugs, and very small children—the kind that cry—are on the plane. Children are always on the plane. I glare at their mothers and fathers. I should have planned better, but those parents are undoubtedly already lamenting a lack of long-range vision that goes back years.

At 5 a.m., the Dallas airport is full of zombies. I mix in with them. Before my layover ends, many of them will have been shipped off to other cities. It's no wonder zombies are such a problem: airports do nothing to stop their spread. I'm still trying to figure out what time it is when I get to Miami, but I have a layover—three hours and thirty-nine minutes—long enough to be a complete bummer but short enough that I can't escape the airport. I hunker down and sulk. After a few breezy hours, my friend AJ, who is joining me on this trip, appears, and we wait in some lines before being herded onto another plane. We fly and fly and fly. We pass the equator. We soar over

Brazil. We curve over the massive sprawl of Buenos Aires and look down on each neighborhood's own soccer pitch—River Plate, Boca Juniors, San Lorenzo de Almagro, Independiente, Racing Club. I think it is Sunday. I think the Seahawks are playing the Steelers. I think I still have one more flight.

After another two hours in the plane, the long air-travel nightmare is over. I have no idea what time it is or even what day. I have lost track of time. It's gone. I think I'm in Argentina, but it doesn't feel like it. It looks and feels like I'm waiting for my bags on a blustery spring day at the Bozeman airport. And just like Bozeman in the springtime, it's cold and overcast in Bariloche, a city of one hundred thousand set in southwestern Argentina's Andean foothills. Conspiracy theorists whisper that Bariloche was the home of Eva Braun and Adolf Hitler after the war. It's an odd thing to hear about a city.

Fly anglers, you can spot them from a mile away: slow walkers ambling through airports in expensive sunglasses, dingy ball caps, and flip-flops. Unshaven, uncombed, and a bit feral, they look like they've just woken up with creaky knees, a dusting of dog hair, and oversized plans for the day. It's the rest of our crew—and everyone is slapping backs and doling out bear-hugs. Along with AJ, whose company imports and sells fly fishing reels, Nick's the photographer, Martin's the guide and our local fixer, and Jay's the hotshot sponsored influencer/angler sent by a rod company to look rugged, catch fish, and do some promotion work for a couple of lodges. I'm on assignment with a strict deadline and vague orders to "write something about Argentina." After the intros, and passing through customs and border control, it takes forever for the team to locate and account for our small mountain of gear—it's the drone, I'm told. It's always an eternity for it to clear security.

I go outside for some fresh air. It still *feels* like Bozeman. Pickups and four-wheel-drive rigs are sprawled over the dusty parking lot. There is scrub-land. The wind lifts fumes of diesel and cow and dust. The trucks don't have Montana tags, however. Instead, they proclaim clearly, "Argentina." It must be true.

Even though I feel like a nasty strip of carpet lying by the highway, I don't tell anyone. I don't even mind that I feel so shitty—I've given up—and if I don't know what time it is, what day it is, or where the hell I am, what does it matter how I'm feeling? It doesn't. Any story I tell myself about how awful and jetlagged I feel is just that—a story. It's a profound moment of self-realization. I flip the script and decide I don't feel all that bad. Bad is relative. Bad is a construct. Bad is not happening. Hell, I can feel pretty good if I resolve to feel good. Why not? It beats the alternative. I start prowling the small *aeropuerto* for my first-ever cold Argentinian cerveza. There are hardly any zombies, I don't see any Nazis, and we have a drone. It's been a long process, but now, finally, it feels something like the beginning of something.

We drive 150 miles northwest across the vastness of Patagonia. It sounds like a long way, but in Argentina—or Montana or Wyoming or Idaho—150 miles ain't shit. It's a warmup. It's a short jog at a leisurely pace. The landscape mirrors the stark places in those big, emptyish Western states—but something is different. Where are the billboards? There are none. The truck stops, chain restaurants, cell-phone towers, outbuildings, and telephone lines—they are just not here. The landscape is free from imposition except for the occasional mysterious roadside shrine bedecked in red garlands, the speck of a shepherd's hut far off in the endless vista, or a lone gaucho on horseback, miles from anything. I settle in. We are not in Bozeman. This really might be Argentina. It really is springtime.

Our first destination is a homey, comfortable lodge tucked into a craggy patch of rock alongside the perky Rio Chimehuin. The massive stratovolcano Lanin is only twenty miles northwest. There are wild horses grazing; gigantic, burly hares who gallop more than they hop; and a sky filled with birds. The dirt around the lodge is not dirt; it is dust the consistency of baby powder—fine volcanic ash from the last time the mighty Lanin had an episode.

We are shown around, introduced to the other guests, and plied with cocktails. Then the inevitable fishing talk begins. As we lean against the split-rail fences, names of the world's hottest hotspots drip from bearded chins like talk of hip downtown brunch spots—the Madison, the Henry's Fork,

South Andros, Iceland, Christmas Island, the Kispiox, the Yellowstone . . . I can only take so much of this puffed-up, been-there, done-that chatter, so AJ and I walk down to the banks of the river just to be close to the water. It is soothing and rejuvenating. Back at the lodge, they start flying the drone. The vultures, wheeling ever higher, pay no mind.

"Now we know what Patagonia looks like," AJ says. He's thinking out loud. Sometimes AJ just wants to talk a bit.

"I think I've seen this before," I say. "I mean, it looks so familiar."

AJ nods and reaches down to put his hand in the water, as if this small gesture will somehow capture Patagonia—give it feeling, make it real. I reach down to touch the water, too. It is very real, indeed.

The drone finally lands and AJ points to a bird. Wherever I go, it's instinctive that I judge a place by which birds hang out there, and in Patagonia, the birds are wonderful. Stoic raptors survey the landscape from canyon crags, songbirds color the air, and even the beloved swallows are there, on vacation from the cold north. It's unlikely, but I wonder if these could be *my* swallows, the ever-sweet tricksters I marvel at along the banks of the Yakima River back in Washington State. Maybe. You never know. Still, it's good to run into an old friend so far from home.

The first day of fishing takes us down the Rio Chimehuin—small, twisting over itself in early-season rush and excitement. "Get a load of that thing," AJ says, pointing toward the bank. "That thing" was a muscular, colorful falcon called the caracara. They are everywhere in Patagonian Argentina, hopping along the ground, out-thugging massive turkey vultures for a share of winter-kill. They are rough, aggressive customers, and our host, Martin, tells us that the fearless birds have knife-like talons—as fearsome as *facons*, the huge, butcher-sized blades usually found lashed inside a gaucho's bright-red belt. "Give 'em some space, amigo. They will tear you up," he warns.

The Rio Chimehuin is a romantic, painterly stream. In a moment, I have my first Patagonian trout. A brown—a big fella—maybe sixteen inches. It took me a long time to get to Patagonia, and somewhere back in time, it took this fish's great, great granddaddy a long time to get here, too. He could have come from California, maybe Germany, perhaps England. The history is still a bit fuzzy as to how trout emigrated to Patagonia, but by the early 1900s, they had a solid foothold in a new land—an ecosystem rich with habitat and sustenance, and nearly devoid of predators. Patagonia was a place the trout, as I had, found familiar—a place they liked so much they decided to throw down roots and call it home.

I say a few words of thanks in Spanish to that first trout —*"Gracias, señor trucha. Hasta luego"*—and slide him back home. It feels good to talk to a fish in its native tongue. It's a milestone, and I crack a Quilmes, Argentina's ubiquitous, fizzy yellow beer. Few things are better than a streamside victory beer after landing an excellent trout, and, to no one's surprise, this sacred law of fly fishing also applies in Argentina.

We stay on the Chimehuin another day, the river widening and growing as it ambles south. The fishing gets better by the hour. It could be the spring sun warming the river, it could be the season's first vigorous eruption of insect life, or it could be the fact that I feel, river mile after river mile, like I've been fishing this water my whole life. I know what's around the next bend. I know where the fish are supposed to be. I know just as much as I need to know.

After fishing, we retire to the lodge for an embarrassing feast of meat, pickled things, cheese, and bottle after bottle of Malbec, Argentina's deliciously inky red wine. I am not used to being pampered. Truth be told, extravagant trips are few and far between for fly fishing writers like me. I'm certainly grateful, but the coddling makes me uneasy. Still, amid all the atypical luxury there are familiar signposts. The dusty pickups in the parking lot, their engines ticking in the shade, look familiar; the crinkly-eyed guides remind me of my angling friends back home; the sun laying light just so along the spine of the Andes makes me think of the Cascades; and the post-fishing jokes are all the same. I have certainly been here before. Patagonia, so far away, now seems so close.

"Do you think these dudes know how to shotgun a beer?" I ask AJ. It is a legitimate question. After all, we are not in Patagonia simply to fish. Everywhere we travel, we have the opportunity to be cultural ambassadors.

It's an unofficial part of the job. I round up an armful of Quilmes while the guides stand in a circle, kicking at the dirt, shooting the shit like guides do everywhere.

AJ is handy with the Spanish. After just a few questions and hand gestures, it's obvious these dudes have never shotgunned a beer. Our opportunity—our duty—is clear. The rules are explained to the guides—Esteban, Marco, and Jamie. We punch holes in the sides of the cans with Esteban's massive Argentinean facon, and we all stand there with goofy smiles of anticipation, waiting for the lodge's chef, Angel, to count down—*Uno, dos, tres . . .*

We drive northeast to the gorgeously empty Mapuche Indian reservation to fish the Rio Malleo, the storied home of Argentinean fly fishing. I step out of the truck, and, again, the feeling is abrupt—I've fished this river before. It's smaller, manageable, and clearly showing off its spring finery. It's the Yakima, the Upper Deschutes, the Crooked, Rock Creek—something small and rambunctious near you. Thousands of miles from home, and it feels like I'm in my backyard—it feels like these are my rivers. It feels like my family. That's an overly sweet way to say it, but the familiarity is so real, so in my face, that I must acknowledge it.

AJ rigs up quickly. "Can you believe this?" he asks. "It's unbelievable. It's the perfect trout stream." He is thinking out loud again, but he's right. I nod my head and smile. I dip my hand in the water. It is believable. It's really real. Springtime in Patagonia.

Somehow, I have angered the fishing gods of the Rio Malleo. If it can go wrong, it already has or is about to. Maybe it's the brand-new rig I'm fishing, because I can't cast. Maybe it's the bug I'm fishing, because the trout hate it. Maybe it's the river, because I've fallen in twice in fifteen minutes. I haven't caught a fish in hours, and I'm staring at an impossibly tangled clusterfuck of leader, tippet, and flies in my hand. I decide to pout on the bank and console myself with the thought that failure is always a better story than success. I watch as AJ catches fish after fish. They are browns. Huge browns. Monsters.

Bigger than anything on the Yakima, Deschutes, Crooked, or Rock Creek. AJ's guide, Marco, slaps him on the back. The photographer gets in close. The light is perfect. The goddamn drone starts to fly overhead. Everyone high-fives. Cue the tango scene.

I've gotten no high-fives and no attaboys. I tell my guide, Esteban, to just leave me alone. I lie down and close my eyes. I feel like Morrissey. Time passes. Nothing happens. I open my eyes, and tiny ants are biting my ankles. It is springtime in Patagonia, and I am melting down.

AJ catches a dozen more fish while I sulk. The guides call lunch, and we amble to a grassy spot for empanadas. In Argentina, lunch is usually empanadas, which is an excellent thing. They are the perfect fishing snack. Compact and tasty, empanadas never get soggy, and there are no tomatoes to get squashed and gross. Go ahead and dunk them in something; they can take it. Wrap one back up in a napkin, bandana, or whatever, and put it in your pocket; it'll be satisfying in an hour or two.

After lunch, it is time for a traditional Argentinean maté, but someone has forgotten the thermos of hot water. No matter. There is a solution: Marco builds a small fire. When the coals are nice and hot, he fills a sixteen-ounce plastic bottle with water. He lays the bottle in the fire just so, and, within a few moments, the water begins to boil. How is the plastic not melting? How is the water boiling? I feel like a caveman seeing his first wheel. It looks like magic, but I am told it has something to do with convection. We make the maté with the magic water and pass the ornate, silver-gilded maté gourd as my swallows wheel above the canyon. The maté is green and strong. After the gourd is drained and refilled a few times, a flask is fished from a dry bag and, with startling suddenness, everything is just like home—again.

But still, there's that fish thing—and the fact that I'm not catching them. I wander to the bank to stare at the water and wonder just what the hell is wrong with me. I can usually avoid that question, but not on this day, not beside this river. Esteban ambles up beside me and puts his arm around my shoulder. I look up at him, squinting into his eyes. In his sweet, tuneful accent, he tells me, "Do not worry about it, *Polako*. In Argentina, just remember that you must ride the burro."

I am trying to understand what this means. I don't know why he's suddenly calling me *Polako*.

"It's your square head and Polish last name. *Polako . . .*"

Esteban points to a vulture, slowly ascending on a thermal. "Look, just take your time, see? It will come. You will get there. Slow is fast. Ride the burro." He squeezes my shoulder, and we stare silently at the vulture, way up there. In a moment, he drifts away without saying another word. As I'm reminded all the time, "profound absurdity" defines fly fishing.

Hidden in cliffs tagged with ancient rock art just south of the tiny village of Pilolil, the second lodge on our agenda overlooks the Rio Alumine. We are the lodge's first-ever guests. Tan and handsome people dressed in white linen and expensive resort wear stand on the porch and welcome us as we straggle in, blinking against the bold spring sun. I imagine they are disappointed by our appearance— they could not have expected this— sunburned, scraggly, barefoot and buzzed on post-fishing beers. They give us hats with the Argentinean flag on the side, push cocktails into our hands, and make the best of it. We meet our hosts, who embody everything I'm falling in love with about Argentina. They are smart, funny, openhearted, curious, and incredibly generous. The lodge is grand and indulgent, but it's still a fishing lodge—though one with a helicopter pad, a massive barbecue pit the size of a small swimming pool, and bidets in every room.

This evening, there is to be a grand inaugural feast, an *asado*, a party. Friends and family have been invited, local dignitaries have been summoned, a baby lamb has been sacrificed, and the victuals are piled up in the kitchen— cheese, fruit, sausages, cold cuts. A staggering amount of food. As the stylishly casual guests trickle in, the guides build a fire in the open pit. It's a rager, and I can feel its heat, even under the late-afternoon sun. It is Thanksgiving Day back home. Here in Argentina, this is a Thursday-night supper.

AJ, however, is not thinking of the food, the drinks, the fish, the river, or our new pals. AJ is thinking about his laundry. He appears with a small pile of damp socks and underpants, and begins hanging them on the grates of the brand-new, gleaming, and elaborate *parrilla*—the stand where our soon-to-be-lamb-dinner will roast.

I don't notice AJ's antics immediately, but Eduardo, the lodge's owner, keeps looking toward the asado, pursing his lips.

Quite casually, AJ is flipping a sock when I run over. "What the hell, man? What are you doing?" I hiss.

"I'm drying my underpants," he says. "What does it look like?"

"It looks like you are drying your goddamn underpants," I say.

He doesn't answer. He defiantly cracks a Quilmes and pokes at the blaze with a stick. I am mortified and aghast. I am embarrassed for AJ, for me, and for all American anglers who will ever fish this lodge in the future. Despite this complete abandonment of appropriate behavior, however, it is pretty funny, and there is really nothing I can do. I walk over to where the guides are standing in a circle, kicking the dirt, chuckling. I try to find the correct phrase in Spanish, *"El está secando* his goddam panties. *¡Dios mio!"*

The Rio Alumine is one of the most remarkable trout streams on the planet. Broad and clear, even in its early-season bustle, it is a hundred rivers contained by a single canyon etched by a massive earth chisel. The Alumine throws wonderment and a series of questions at an angler every foot of every river mile. It is tireless in its range, diversity, and surprise, and from the front of a driftboat, those surprises appear around every river bend.

My first fish is an enormous brown. Big. Even bigger than that. He comes from nowhere, crushing a streamer splashed tight to the bank. My heart stops for a moment when he turns on the fly. We all see the chase. Then he is on. Then the fight, the cheering, the backslapping. I release him. There is glory for El Polako—but then nothing happens. Nothing keeps happening. The river, so gorgeous, is suddenly not giving up the goods. Fish—giant

Patagonian monsters—should be there, and there and there, but they are not. Where the hell are they? We stop for lunch, and I hunt around random coolers for a stray Quilmes. Then I notice it. Unbelievable. A gaffe more egregious than AJ's laundry debacle—a bunch of bananas sit brown and squashy in tepid cooler water. I point into the cooler and yell, "Bananas!"

Everyone stops. Everyone looks. There they are, real as day and tragic as sin. Bananas. In the cooler. On a fishing trip. In Argentina. Monsterland. Springtime. The Alumine. What? How?

I am not superstitious. I don't read my horoscope. I'm not into metaphysics or religion or lottery tickets. But some things are beyond science. Bananas in a boat—thought by sailors to bring bad luck going back to the 1700s, when trade ships that wrecked in the Caribbean were found to be survived only by bananas floating in the water—are one of those things. Do they have this sort of science in Argentina? Are things different here?

No. Universal angling laws are universal angling laws. Bananas in a boat are a definite no-go in Patagonia, too. The guides are humiliated. How could this happen with a drone droning, El Polako catching his big brown, and the gringo who dries his underpants on the asado? Esteban calls a meeting with his crew. Something must be done. After some shouting, pointing, and hugging, the plan is in place. We are to smash the bananas with rocks, yell an insult regarding bananas, and then chuck them into the Rio Alumine. Everyone has to do it; everyone does. While this scene is happening, I think, "Is this really happening?"

After lunch, AJ begins throwing streamers and I switch to an oversized, dry attractor pattern. We pound the bank. Fish, suddenly, are where they are supposed to be. Two massive rainbows battle over one perfectly cast streamer. A twenty-three-inch brown sips the dry as delicately as a kitty lapping a bowl of milk. There are giant fish. There are doubles. Trout porn is happening all around us, and we can only wonder: Was it the bananas? Esteban smiles and says, "You just had to wait. You just had to climb on the burro!"

On our final day in Patagonia, we have a decision to make: hit a small, unfished spring creek we may or may not have access to, or roll over to Lago Tromen, a lake at the very base of Volcan Lanin. I vote for the spring creek. I lose. The lake it is.

Lago Tromen is too beautiful, like a painting by a nature artist who has yet to realize that nature is not supposed to be perfect in every detail. But Lago Tromen is truly perfect, and holds massive brown, rainbow, and brook trout. We bomb long casts to the bank, over drop-offs and into shady cover. At one point, we wade a hard sand bottom and wait for hungry trout to emerge, patrolling the flat like bonefish. It is not like actual fishing. It is too good. It is too much. It is overwhelming. No fish less than sixteen inches. Not a bum fight on the fight card. Not a moment when I don't look around in awe. Lanin, the massive volcano, looms above us. I think, "vast." I think, "Mount Rainier." I think, "home" and "backyard." I am beginning to understand.

We motor back and load the boats, and then I jump in a pickup that reminds me of my beater back home. Along the way, we get a flat. A stranger stops and helps us fix it. I try to tell a joke in Spanish and fail, but the guides laugh anyway. A few beers are left in one of the coolers, and we drink them by the side of the dirt road, in the middle of nothing, in the middle of every-thing, in the middle of springtime.

RIVER SONG

The Great Debates

George Washington's teeth weighed more than four pounds.

The dimensions of Fenway Park are 310 feet to left, 420 to the deepest part of center field, and 302 down the right field line.

The state bird of Montana is the western meadowlark.

If one were to stack a billion one-dollar bills on top of one another, the pile would be sixty-three miles tall.

Polar bears can run twenty-five miles an hour, are able to jump more than six feet in the air, and are nearly undetectable by infrared cameras due to their transparent fur.

The speed of sound in water is 3,348 miles per hour.

The conterminous United States extends 2,897 miles from ENE to WSW, and 2,848 miles from SSE to NNW.

It is possible to assign every US president a trout fly that best suits his administration.

Whether steelheading, trout fishing, or elk hunting, you'll hear these sorts of things sitting around a campfire. Without the aid of cell towers and search engines, these sorts of campfire pronouncements would take forever to be resolved—which they rarely are. Arguments could drag on for days. It could get shouty, even heated. And even with instant facts at your fingers, some debates—the nonfactual tussles involving taste or opinion—are eternal, rising every year around the firepit. These are the flames that never die—Gordie Howe vs. Wayne Gretzky; mesquite vs. cherry wood; brand, model, and year of particular pickup trucks; and, of course, streamer fishing vs. every other kind of fishing.

And while the range of stupid things we argue about includes all manner of science, sports, history, music, movies, and names of constellations, a few things remain sacrosanct. We never talk religion or politics—and, just to be safe, girlfriends, wives, mamas, and relationships are strictly off-limits, too.

Despite how testy some of these discussions can get (I'm loyal to Ford Rangers until my dying day), the ground rules work, and in more than twenty years of road-tripping with these old pals, hurt feelings are rare and actual dustups have only occurred on a couple of occasions.

This year, I rode out with Foghorn. I've known the guy since college and, thanks to hours spent in the car, know that he drinks a Diet Pepsi upon rising, followed by a can of Rainier ("To balance my chi"). He dips Skoal Long Cut, listens to the Rancid album *And Out Come the Wolves* while he waders up, and only smokes his salmon with cherry wood. Most importantly, since he's from Michigan, he sides with me on the Howe vs. Gretzky debate. Howe all the way.

Foggy and I crushed it this fall. We exercised big browns on the Beaverhead, skirted the low water on the Big Hole to feed hungry pods of grayling, rainbows, and browns, and stuck big, dumb cutts everywhere on Rock Creek.

For late fall, the weather was perfect—warm days, frosty nights, and just enough chill in the air to inspire a bit of urgency in the trouts' feeding pattern. It was that perfect window when golden cottonwoods shiver in the breeze, and the smoke from the summer's forest fires finally starts to dissipate, but the tangy bite of woodsmoke still hangs in the air.

Foghorn and I were leapfrogging up the banks of the Big Hole River in southwest Montana, finding fish in all the places fish should be. The big boys finned at the top of pools claiming first dibs on whatever floated through. Behind them were gangs of smaller fish, followed by the occasional grayling and the ever-lurking mountain whitefish. Trout were hunkered behind likely-looking boulders, hugging the inside of bends and cut banks, hanging in the seam, laying low at the bottom of tailouts. Textbook.

More impressive than the number of fish was the fact that we were catching them. I was taking fish below on a two-pheasant-tail rig (pheasant tails, by the way, equal President Hoover because of their ability to vacuum the bottom of a stream) while Foggy was using an orange stimulator (Trump) and a Quigley cripple (Franklin Roosevelt).

The fish were coming so readily that the casting became leisurely. Instead of racing upstream from pool to riffle, we took our time. We watched each other land fish, spotted songbirds, chewed jerky, and stared at the clouds. It was perfect.

"I've realized something about fishing," Foghorn said as we kicked up the stream into a gorgeous meadow section.

"What's that?"

"Well," he said, "it's not really so much about fishing specifically, but when you are out here and it's so damned beautiful and you are grabbing trout . . . well, it just feels totally excellent to be really good at something. I just feel grateful."

This simple, heartfelt statement hit me like a bolt. I just nodded and smiled. But my old pal was right in so many ways. Imagine not fishing. Imagine no road trips. No old friends. No fires. No preposterous, full-throated arguments about how many stars are contained by the Milky Way (between two hundred and four hundred billion). What would you do? On that amazing fall day, standing on the banks of the Big Hole, I couldn't fathom an answer.

For once, Foghorn would get no argument from me.

8

HOPE

What do we expect out of this fly fishing thing, really? No angler anticipates perfection. We've all long abandoned that pipedream. Facing the cold stone of reality, we can't trust that somehow, against everything we have ever witnessed, the fishing gods will be fair to us. We cannot even have faith in moderate success. That is all too much.

The only thing a fisher can aspire to cultivate is one pure and simple thing: garden-variety hope. Hope as a small coal that never goes out. Hope as a pole star. Hope as a life raft. Hope as that tiny bit of comfort that somehow propells us through the thick of a salmon marathon—forty-five days of relentless fishing, forty-five days of early mornings, forty-five days of no fish, wrong tide, too crowded, too much seaweed, too windy, too something or other. Hope as only itself: Hope. As anglers, we've earned it, and we cling to it like a life raft. It's ours.

The every-other year run of pink salmon in the Salish Sea is always a good time. A few years ago it was better than good. It was off the charts—the most prodigious showing since Washington State started counting them. Somewhere close to seven million fish were projected to swim by western Washington's beaches. Locals were jacked up and tying gaudy flies in the fish's favorite color—hot pink. The local sporting goods stores were picked clean of pink jigs, pink Buzz Bombs, pink spinners. Pink, pink, pink. Everything pink. Local barstool talk centered on the big pink run two years prior when anglers were the unlikely heroes of the beaches, often outfishing gear chuckers two-to-one. Would this year be the same?

So what if pinks are the smallest species of salmon? So what if some salmon snobs think they are of a lower class or don't taste as good, or don't battle as hard or carry the same sort of cachet as their cousins? They take flies. They fight in a whirling dervish of self-preservation. They like to hang around Seattle. Good enough for the fly chuckers I know.

As summer eased into autumn, we rehashed the sessions we'd had on the Duwamish River channel, just south of downtown Seattle in the shadow of cement plants, rebar mills, dry docks, and shipyards. Would the mysterious and baffling oracle controlling the Washington Department of Fish and Wildlife open the channel to fishing again this year? We crossed our fingers and waited for the regulations to be published.

A former home to the Duwamish Tribe's longhouses, smoking fires, and an enormous armada of dugout canoes, the channel is now a federal Superfund site and the very definition of a wasted industrial waterway. Once called *tohl-AHL-too* ("herring house") and later *hah-AH-poos* ("where there are horse clams"), our local pink-salmon hotspot was one of the largest Native American settlements in the Pacific Northwest. Thought to have been inhabited since around the sixth century, this intertidal area has but one natural bend left, but in the folds of that last unstraightened, unchanneled half-mile of urban river, the pinks return in huge numbers. We drag pontoons over land that Chief Sealth himself surely stalked, while we dodge tugs, barges, and freighters to cast over the most willing of salmon. Remember that day last run, someone asks, when we were just herding them up and down the channel? Yes. We remember. We all remember.

Before the pinks (also known as "humpies"—for the dorsal hump that appears on spawning males) ascend the local rivers to spawn, they gorge close to local beaches. One of the most productive beaches in the Northwest is ten minutes from my house by car, and then a ten-minute walk from the parking lot to the point where I like to cast. In the early-morning loaming, the air, the mist, the rocks smell wet and metallic, like a bag of pennies. The fog blurs the line between sea and sky, erasing the horizon. The gulls wheel and bitch; out in the mist, a sea lion barks. Light change. Tide change. Gentle winds. Everything is just right. Hope.

According to the catch card provided by the State of Washington, I caught my first pink on August 4. It was still early in the season, and the beach was populated only by locals: Cherie, the pugnacious day trader who stands all of 5'2" and her husband, Wayne, the best gear chucker on the beach. Ted, the Duwamish, wearing his shell necklace imbued with some power to which I had no access. Earl, the dude from Maine who'd done time for setting illegal traplines. Ray the Rasta, always in sandals and shorts no matter the weather. And, of course, the three or four rotating fly fishers. Some had excellent casts; some struggled to get the line out. Long casts are the key to beach fishing for pinks, and short casts point to long, fishless days.

Whether an angler is chucking gear or tossing flies in the salt, upon hooking a pink, the technique is the same: set the hook, play the fish, and when, finally, the fish tires and gets close to the shore, tighten up and sprint up the cobbled beach to high ground, dragging the salmon from the grasp of the dangerous breakers. From there, the "driftwood shampoo" is administered, and the fish is bled, gutted, and cleaned. The gulls get the guts, the cooler gets the fish, and the occasional tourist gets a show. It is a gory business, and by the end of the month, I'd harvested fifteen salmon and my waders were tattooed with blood splotches that would never come out.

No matter how often it is done, killing a salmon is not light-duty. Dragged heaving onto the beach, these fish have battled for their lives, and a few well-placed whacks with a hunk of driftwood seems an ignoble way for them to go. With every fish I catch, I wish there were some way to honor them, along with the Duwamish people, whose home waters the salmon return to and whose beach I fish. It seems like I should do something— build a fire under the moon; whisper their ancient and forgotten name— *h?dú?*—into the breeze; sing to them.

In the moments between fish, staring at the horizon, I think about time— time counted in fish runs, time counted by moon cycles, time counted in generations. It's humbling and leads to the inevitable thoughts about the intertwined fates of these fish and those people who called this beach home. Those are bitter thoughts, and the words that surround them—erasure, displacement, extinction, holocaust—are the ugliest in our language. I have my own ritual. After the season's first fish is killed, I slit it's gills and then slice open the belly. The heart is usually still beating, even as I hold it in my hands. I close my eyes and eat the gift. It's some sort of communion, I guess.

By the end of the month, the fish were in heavy. I recorded two on August 27; four on August 29; six on August 30. Now the fish were everywhere—in the rivers, on the beaches, in the industrial waterway. Driving over the West Seattle Bridge, I'd almost stray into oncoming traffic, distractedly attempting to spot rising fish in the estuary below.

I had tried to convince myself that I'd fish every day—every damn day— for as long as the fish were there. It was a heady idea and would make for a great magazine article. It didn't pan out. It became a position I had never applied for—load the pontoon, unload the pontoon, row, fish, row. Drive to the beaches, walk to the points, fish, fish, fish. As a writer, I am more than allergic to any notion that whispers j-o-b, so, out of obstinate reflex, I ended up sitting out a few days. Still, every day I skipped the beach or the boat etched pangs of guilt into the back of my hunter-gatherer brain.

By the peak of the run, Foghorn was a regular at my house. My old fishing buddy would make the drive up from Portland with a case of beer, some jerky, and his dog, Mr. Pants. Even though my go-to beach had now been overrun by regular Joes out to stock the larder, Foggy, intent on squeezing in as much fishing as possible over a weekend, drove me like a muleskinner. We'd fish my new, no-tell-um strand in the morning, stop off at the local brewery, damp and stinking in our waders for a victory beer at noon, and hit the channel or the river after a nap. Eight, sometimes ten hours of fishing a day. It all started to swirl together save for those unexpected moments: an abandoned baby harbor seal nuzzling our pontoons looking for his mama; dogfish sharks and ratfish swimming at our feet looking for fish guts; an osprey out on his morning hunt; bald eagles whirling and calling over us; the eight-hundred-pound sea lion picking fish off the end of our lines as we god-dammed in fear and amazement, white-knuckling the frames of our pontoons.

By the end of August, there were thirty-five fish in the freezer and it was time to smoke. Foggy and I stayed up into the wee hours, cleaning, brining, carefully cutting off the fatty, delicious belly strips. At 2 a.m., stereo blaring, I was the Iron Salmon Chef, whipping out Thai-flavored salmon; whisky-and-brown-sugar salmon; salmon sushi; salmon stew; salmon collar with miso. We were delirious. There was glory all around, and hope was no longer needed; it was now something for fishers other than us, lesser fishers, fishers who didn't have millions of hungry salmon hanging around their neighborhood. We smoked the fish in three or four huge batches, setting up a production line and blowing out an almost-new vacuum sealer in the midst of it.

The fish kept coming. September 2: six fish; September 3: four fish; September 5: three fish. September 11 brought Foggy's fourth trip in as many weeks. There was a permanent imprint of his body on my couch, and he had his own section of the fridge where he kept his beer, salami, and sardines. After forty-some fish, the local bartenders had seen me more in waders than in street clothes, and both pairs of waders could stand by themselves. I didn't want the season to be winding down, but at the same time, I was bone-tired. But goddammit, they were still out there. What was hope now? Hope was a long nap.

The last spurt of fish came toward the middle of September. I made it out to the beach less and less, and abandoned the waterway after the local Tribes set their nets for the more valuable silver salmon, which follow the pinks like morning follows night. I met a girl and spent some of my newly found free time listening to her sing pretty folk songs. It is amazing what time, when you have it again, can offer.

I'll get back out to the beach and start casting for silvers any day now, and after them, the huge, brawling chum. After them, the near impossibility of winter steelhead. The excavation of hope, with its new meanings, its new glint, commences again.

Concrete and Barbed Wire

You're trespassing. You need to get off this river, son.
    Why?
'Cause it's my property.
    Where'd you get it?
Was my daddy's.
    Where'd he get it?
From his father.
    Where'd he get it?
He fought for it.
    Who'd he fight?
Lotsa folk.
    Who?
Goes way back.
    That how this works? We can fight for it? Now?

9

BURNING PRAM

"Drink the wild air."

—RALPH WALDO EMERSON

If you've spent more than just a few afternoons at it, you know that fly fishing is a relentlessly solitary sport and that, ultimately, we all fish alone, our only companion, the ever-chattering brain. But fly angling is an activity that perfectly separates that brain (I calculate, scheme, and strategize) from its body (I see, cast, strike) so that we can glimpse their clear, inseverable connections in remarkable detail as if for the first time. It's akin to washing a season's worth of road grime off your pickup and being charmed by the notion that the old beater just happens to sport your favorite shade of faded emerald-green.

As autumn began to give way to Seattle's "big dark," I needed the solitary reflection of the river but also the company of friends, and I needed them both badly. I had just lost a rare, well-paying writing gig. Work on my novel had stalled. My bank account was wheezing, the bill pile seemed close to avalanche, and I needed a brake job on my truck and five hundred gallons of heating oil for the winter. There really wasn't much in the weighing of the decision. I gathered the gear, loaded up the dogs, pointed the truck east, and prayed the old girl would make it over the pass just one more time.

Stepping into a river does something to our brains. Usually, as I approach the stream, my mind is close to overflowing its banks, juggling dozens of intertwined observations, schemes, memories, and ideas—a perfect wind knot of thoughts. It seems impossible to hold so many plans, designs, and bits of internal dialogue and still be able to focus enough to tie on a fly. Yet, as I settle into the casting and retrieving, the mind also begins to recede. After a time, the impossible jumble begins to evaporate. Some of what remains is related to the fishing, but most of it is not—a melody from a horrible 1980s pop song, an annoying TV jingle, the lines of a strongly worded email never sent to an old boss. Finally, the cascade calms and thoughts slow to a trickle. There is a new, delightful, and surprising focus, and I am thinking, if I'm particularly lucky that day, one pure thing. That is the brand of concentration that sets fire to my perceptions. By "unthinking," I automatically see more. I hear the cool whisps over the water, smell the aroma of sage rolling down from the canyon walls, communicate with that dipper jumping from rock to rock. Movement becomes simple: action and reaction, anticipation, instinct. It's too much to label it a Buddhism of the predator. Still, there is no denying the meditative intensity of this state. We call it, for lack of a better term, "the zone."

If there is a competing thought in my head, a crystal-clear sense of awareness often proclaims simply, loudly, "I love this. There is no replacement for now. I am lucky to be here. I am alive." For an angler, "this" is what "it" is all "about."

Still, as solitary as fly fishing is at its core, that deep dive toward the zone requires a fully engaged support system. This is why fly fishing is built upon camaraderie in a way few other activities on Earth can match.

A fine walk streamside, the shedding of extraneous brain activity, and catching the occasional fish are all fine and good, but in many ways, I am not only there for solitary fishing. I'm there to rejoice in my friends, buddies, pals, and family—adopted or otherwise. I seek to commune with those who've climbed over the wall and goofed around in the zone for an afternoon, a weekend, a lifetime. Simply stated, as fly anglers, we go to awesome places with our friends and make friends with places that are awesome.

⸺

I fight back gnawing impatience as I navigate the brake-light drive from Seattle over Snoqualmie Pass and finally into the Yakima River Canyon. The river runs through a sage-scented gorge framed by columnar basalt and populated by rattlesnakes, osprey, bighorn sheep, trout, grouse, and chucker. This weekend is a harvest festival, and fly anglers come from all the big, squarish states—Washington, Idaho, Wyoming, Colorado, Montana, even Oregonians are allowed to share in the abundance. For a crew of Northwest anglers, these are the High Holy Days of the fishing year.

The specific locale doesn't matter, of course. The same meetups occur like seasonal migrations along the Madison in Montana, in the Driftless Area in Wisconsin, on some beach off the Gulf Coast, or somewhere a good half-day's drive from Denver, Boise, or Detroit. We gather to celebrate the thing—the one thing—with our like-minded kinfolk.

They are called rondis, gatherings, get-ups, or shakedowns—or here in Central Washington, Burning Pram.

⸺

The clouds color and a pumpkin moon begins its slow creep over the canyon rim as the massive bonfire begins to secure its hold in the center of the campground. This signals the beginning of the night's activities. We all know what's just around the corner. Thirty-some dogs of all size, age, shape, and variety strain at their collars as their handlers marshal them toward the starting line. The track is laid out, defined by Mexican *veladoras* candles, garage-sale votives, and LED headlamps. Finally, all is set. One of Burning Pram's most revered traditions—the all-breed dog race—is about to commence.

The command is given to clear the track, and a hush falls over spectators. The signal sounds, and the hounds are off! All that dog flesh, all that enthusiasm, thundering willy-nilly down the fifty-yard BLM parking-lot straightaway is so improbable, so random that it seems a force of nature. The spectacle is adorably goofy, a tiny bit majestic, and utterly ridiculous. Now it's Dog who has the earnestly focused mind—the glory of the finish line—while humans lose theirs for a few delirious moments, leaping and howling under the influence of an enthused pack of mutts and a handful of just-rising stars.

The night stumbles forward. We greet friends with immense bear-hugs and heroic slugs of the moonshine brewed up by a welder from Eugene. The photographer from Portland passes out new-baby cigars while the nurse from Spokane pours sloppy glugs of expensive Washington Syrah and Oregon Pinot Noir into battered tin cups. G-Man has been roping cutts in the Yellowstone backcountry since his wife left him in July. Fat Mike is all packed for the East Cape to see if he can put the sneak on a rooster fish. Jimbo got a bit too close to a griz up in Alaska. And Jay-Jay and his new setter, Stella, brought some pheasant capes from his last scattergun trip to Dakota.

Frozen, vac-packed, and cured delicacies are pulled from coolers. Everyone, it seems, has some smoked salmon, but there are also great hunks of venison and elk roasting over coals, wild mushroom soup bubbling on a camp stove, and veggie chili getting a topping of garden-grown Walla-Walla onions and a splash of blistering habanero sauce. Another keg of homebrew begins to drain.

Still to come, of course, is the annual rock/paper/scissors tournament. There is fire jumping and the burning of the crudely crafted sacrificial fishing pram that gives the weekend its name. Later, the guitars come out. Someone sings "This Land is Your Land," which improbably segues into "Louie Louie." Unexpected performance art springs up beside the massive campfire. A joy pervades the entire campground—it is unbounded, palpable, and you can just about smell the mischief and freedom in the air. Everyone is in the zone.

It takes a while for the last of the crew to call it a night—winning this party is a point of pride. And just a few moments after the final warrior has surrendered to sleep, the first of the early risers are up to begin feeding the crowd pancakes, bacon-fried cinnamon rolls, and scratch Bloody Marys.

———

Fly fishing is a ridiculous activity filled with staggering amounts of failure, self-inflicted beatdowns, and frustration. Yet, we soldier on, ignoring the sunburnt humiliations, shivering dunks, and gale-force skunkings. The only way to survive, mind intact, is to laugh at fly fishing's impossibilities and squeeze the joy not only from our accomplishments, but from our shared humility in the face of such long odds. And it's this sort of celebration that makes a thing like Burning Pram not only a wondrous part of the sport but an inevitable one. We share in ways that are automatic, absolute, and genuine, and try not to muck the thing up with overthinking.

Sunday, after camp is broken, I find myself struck: Why, sometimes in what we call "real life," are we ashamed of such joy, of such love? Why must we invent reasons like Burning Pram to reclaim connections that are as indispensible as breathing? And why is it that sometimes, on crisp October weekends along the verges of a gorgeous river in absolute autumn swagger, those questions seem so absurdly foreign as to be laughable?

I loaded the dogs (second and third in the big race!) in the old green rig, pointed her toward the pass, toward the bills, toward the brake jobs and smiled to myself, for myself, and had one pure thought: "This is as good as it gets."

Eat the Rich

The world's fattest skinny man is served
two eight-inch poached trout
in a Gewürztraminer reduction
over mint, watercress, and shelled baby peas.
Poached? that seems odd to me . . .
This is the Firehole, sir.
True.
Is there something wrong, sir?
I just remembered, I'm not fond of trout.

10

GATHER WHITE STONES

The Hornbrook Chevron looks like any other place to buy gas, road snacks, and fishing licenses along northern California's I-5 corridor. It seems to be one of the only businesses still standing in tiny Hornbrook (population 286). Locals linger to chat while a stream of motorists pause for a fill-up and a stretch. Just a few hundred yards away, California State Route 96 begins its twisting, indirect route west, running side by side with the Klamath River.

In the Chevron parking lot, I meet wild fish activist and filmmaker Mikey Wier and longtime CalTrout staffer Andrew Braugh. Mikey wears the bemused grin and thousand-yard stare that betrays years spent chasing trout and salmon throughout the world. Andrew, CalTrout's Mount Shasta/Klamath regional director, has an eager smile that emits energy and earnestness. We lean against his drift boat and hash out the day's plans.

The lot is the unofficial rendezvous point for fly fishing trips on the upper Klamath. It's the place where guides meet sports, where coffee chases donuts, and where strategies are hatched. As we're chatting, a trucker ambles over. He's seen the drifter and wants to talk fishing. Everyone here wants to talk fishing, and after the usual exchange of semi-current fishing reports, I ask if there's any news to share about Iron Gate Dam, just nine miles up the road. The trucker shrugs. "I just don't know," he says. "I really don't, but I do want to see these fish do well."

The aging Iron Gate Dam is owned by Warren Buffett's PacifiCorp power company. It and three other upriver dams are the high-profile center of a whirling, multi-level dam removal debate. The stakeholders are diverse— Tribes, multinational corporations, ranchers, environmentalists, anglers, the government—and nuts-and-bolts, who-gets-what issues such as energy costs, Tribal rights, irrigation allotments, and preserving an ecosystem and species are on the table . . . or the chopping block. But as this parking lot proves once again, dam controversy or not, it will always be true: nobody hates salmon.

It's a perfect fall morning. The drive to the boat launch is delicious. Like every drive to begin a fishing trip, it takes forever. Along the way, we pass homes (cozy), campgrounds (half-full) and restaurants (closed). There are few anglers—too few. A day like this should see the river teeming with activity. I also see the first of what would be a common sight during this trip—a green State of Jefferson flag flapping in the wind.

Decades-old, the State of Jefferson secessionist movement regained momentum during the Trump era. Anti-tax, anti-regulation, pro-gun, pro-militia, and staunchly libertarian, the campaign seeks to establish the rural counties around the California/Oregon border as a separate state. The flags are an unsubtle reminder of Trumpism and its grievances. When it comes to removing the Klamath River dams, Jefferson Staters are an ornery "no."

But would they say yes to saving some money? According to a study by public utilities commissions in Oregon and California, PacifiCorp customers would save more than $100 million by bringing the Klamath River dams down rather than spending more than $500 million to bring them up to modern standards.

———

Rivers cannot help but be beautiful. It takes considerable time, money, and will to despoil one. Rivers are also as resilient as they are beautiful, and perhaps that strength can withstand the assaults we subject them to. The Klamath is flat-out gorgeous. From its start in Oregon's high desert to its broad mouth emptying into the Pacific Ocean in northern California, its route describes a way of life for those lucky enough to live near it. Along its course, it is used for irrigation, energy, drinking water, and recreation. It is also the home to salmon, steelhead, bull trout, rainbow trout, coastal cutthroat trout, and Pacific lamprey. These fish are the physical and spiritual lifeblood of the Yurok, Karuk, Hoopa Valley, Shasta, and Klamath Tribes, who have lived on its banks forever.

Iron Gate Dam is not beautiful. It looks like most dams—gurgling black froth, attended to by seagulls and decorated with pipes and pumps and heavy machinery, seeping the smell of ozone and diesel. When you get close, the brutalist structure hums—an ominous, barely perceptible drone that never stops. "I just call it the goddamn dam," says Mikey.

Completed in 1964, Iron Gate is the lowest dam on the Klamath. It's an earthen embankment standing 173 feet tall and 540 feet wide. Its two turbines can generate 112,650,000 kilowatt-hours of electricity, roughly enough to power around 10,000 homes for a year. In comparison, a typical 2-megawatt wind turbine can provide electricity for about 400 homes yearly.

Standing at the midpoint of the Klamath, the dam is, effectively, the end of the road for fish. It was built without any way for salmon and steelhead to get over or around, slamming the door on their attempts to reach spawning habitat upriver. As a futile effort toward mitigation, the Iron Gate Fish Hatchery has released about one million Chinook salmon yearlings and up to twelve million Chinook salmon fingerlings annually since 1980. Additionally, the hatchery dumps approximately two hundred thousand steelhead yearlings into the river each year. Perched beside a beautiful river, the hatchery is a glum slab of architecture. Even the picnic area seems gloomy.

Aside from being a dead end for salmon, Iron Gate signifies a dividing line between civilization and wilderness. Below the dam, there are fields to irrigate, homes to light.

We gear up, assemble rods, and pick out flies. Mikey and Andrew run the shuttle. I wander around below the dam, trying to get a sense of the place.

There is little activity at the hatchery; a few maintenance trucks sit in the lot, and that's it. I make my way back down to the river, where I run across two anglers visiting from Colorado. They've hired a local outfitter to guide them for the day. The forecast? Fair. The run of king salmon has mostly petered out—only a few battered strays ghost through the pools. As for steelhead, maybe. There are reports of scattered sightings. But trout—there are always trout.

The anglers take a few selfies by the sun-speckled drifter, joke, peer at fly boxes—regular boat launch stuff. Before I can even bring up the subject, one of the guys jerks his thumb over his shoulder. "Hopefully, when we come back in a year or two, that dam will be gone. This may be the last time we have to look at it."

By the time Mikey and Andrew get back and our boat hits the water, the sun is up, erasing the fall morning's chill. It doesn't take long before we find a trout, then another and another. The early success is a pressure-release valve, freeing the mind to think about things other than fishing. Andrew is eager to talk about his work on the river.

His job is to build relationships with the basin's ranchers and farmers—the stakeholders most interested in a reliable water flow. The goal is to implement water management improvements to help them control their irrigation more efficiently while restoring habitat in the tributaries crossing their land. It's not glamorous, but it's emblematic of the painstaking, boots-on-the-ground, behind-the-scenes effort it takes to preserve wild water and wild fish. "In the rural West," Andrew explains, "there is a real fear that environmentalists are out there to take the water or sue you and put you out of business. Perceived or real is beside the point. We have to counter that fear and offer real solutions."

For CalTrout, it's been a productive effort that leans into engineering, real-world economics, and what Andrew calls "kitchen table" talk. "We have to demonstrate that we understand their point of view," he explains. "If you can't establish a rapport, you're not going to get through the front gate, let alone get to the kitchen table to talk about real, constructive solutions."

For Andrew, CalTrout must confront the fears and misinformation ranchers and farmers face. "The important thing to remember," he says, "is that they see themselves as stewards of the land, too. But they also don't want to pass down a ranch that's under litigation or facing the threat of being shut down. If you can reduce that fear, it changes how they think about their entire future. Nobody hates salmon."

When not fretting about potential litigation, ranchers are deeply concerned about utility costs. For CalTrout, rising rates are a conversation starter. By modernizing operations, ranchers and farmers save money. "If there's meaningful value for them, they'll listen, and we can parley that into meaningful environmental change," Andrew explains.

That change doesn't come quickly, but all that talking could be paying off. "We know how to grow cows, but we don't know how to grow fish," says fifth-generation cattle rancher Blair Hart. "But we're gonna learn." With the help of CalTrout, the Hart Ranch is becoming a model of efficient water management, opening more than ten miles of habitat on the Little Shasta River. "To keep this legacy ranch intact—which has been in our family for 168 years—the only way to meet regulatory demands coming from society is to become efficient," says Hart. On the Cardoza Ranch, about an hour away, a similar project has opened fourteen miles of habitat on the Parks Creek tributary.

After the regulation post-game analysis (plenty of trout, no steelhead) Mikey and I hit the road. California State Route 96 follows the Klamath, rambling southwest and crossing the Tribal lands of the Hoopa, Karuk, and Yurok. It also includes what's known as the Bigfoot Scenic Highway, where the most Bigfoot sightings in the country occur.

While 96 is undoubtedly a breathtaking drive through northern California's most remote parts, the area is struggling. Along the river's banks, people have been battered by a triple whammy of calamity. Yearly fires have devastated homes, businesses, and communities. Covid-19 ravaged the region, killing indiscriminately but cutting through Tribal lands with brutal, unflinching horror. Finally, the economic realities in the area are harsh. Unemployment, bankruptcies, homelessness, and drug addiction have been cruel, quick, and deadly in these communities. It seems so hard to fathom—a galloping river, a redwood forest set against a crisp autumn day, yet along Route 96, there is sadness, fear, confusion.

We stop on a bridge at the confluence of the Scott and Klamath Rivers. Mikey's steelhead senses are tingling, and he thinks we might see some fish stacked up, waiting to ascend the Scott. Small, clear, and picture-perfect, the Scott is a crucial spawning tributary of the Klamath. If the Scott is sick, the Klamath feels the symptoms and steelhead and salmon suffer the consequences.

As predicted, there are fish in the pool, but the water is too low for them to begin their dash to the spawning grounds. They fin in the clear, deep pool, their noses pressed into the small waterfall leading to the Scott. More than a hundred fish are waiting. We stare out over them, astonished by the abundance, worried for them.

Next to the pool, a rock juts out, offering a promontory just below the waterfall. The stones are worn smooth, and I realize it's the perfect place to hook, net, or snag those fish. You could practically reach down and grab one. How long have people stood on that rock, watching the ancestors of these salmon? How long does it take to wear down a stone? How old is old?

We're glued to the scene, wondering out loud about the fish, admiring them, when Marty Driskell joins us on the bridge. Retired, Marty is an enthusiastic fisherman who spends his time on the waters of southern Oregon and northern California. He spied us peering into the water, and his steelhead senses started tingling, too. He talks about fish runs of the past—the good years, the bad years, and finally, what's happening right before our eyes. "This is horrible," he says. "There just isn't enough water."

I pepper Marty with questions about the fish, the dams, what this river could be with abundant runs. He doesn't have many answers. Marty just wants to talk about fishing. But what about that dam, I press. What happens if it comes down? Marty turns to me and shrugs. "I just don't know how they'll get power to everybody."

As we drive through the forest, we pass tiny hamlets, marked by ghosts of mom-and-pop motels, diners, and throwback tourist traps. After a few more miles a crumbling chamber of commerce sign greets us: "Welcome to Happy Camp. Klamath River—Steelhead Capital of the World." It's obviously an unsanctioned title disputed by many.

Happy Camp, the headquarters of the Karuk Tribe, has seen happier days. The surrounding peaks are still blackened by horrific burns left from 2020's record-setting wildfire season. You can trace the paths of the Slater and Devil Fires as they rushed toward the town's main street. By the time the flames were finally doused after two months, more than 166,000 acres were torched, 158 homes had burned to the ground, a dozen people were injured, and two firefighters had lost their lives. The fire left half the town homeless.

"We couldn't see across Main Street because of the smoke," Daniel Effman, owner of Partner's Deli and Arcade, tells us. "People were hiding along the river bank to escape the fires coming down."

But these situations, tragic as they are, bring out the best in people, especially in small, tight-knit communities like Happy Camp. From his deli, Daniel immediately began offering free food to his neighbors. "Your money's no good in Happy Camp," he told them.

When we stop for lunch, Daniel asks us if we are fishing, if we've had any luck. I ask about the river, the salmon, and the dams. "They say if the dams go down, we'll be walking across the river—no water. But some people say if the dams go down, it'll be good for the salmon spawning, so I don't know."

On its route to the sea, the Klamath is fed by hundreds of streams, creeks, and tributaries, each vying for the most beautiful vista. One of the river's main tributaries is the nineteen-mile-long Salmon River. It is pristine and undammed, and as we get closer, Mikey's steelhead senses start tingling again. We turn off 96 and point the truck upriver to explore a spot he knows.

This area is considered ancient Karuk tribal land, and on the bridge that crosses the river a few miles from its confluence with the Klamath, there can be no mistake. The structure is tagged "Indian Pride," the hashtag #landback stands out in black spray paint. Next to "This Is Native Land," someone has carefully rendered the Karuk word "OOK" (here) with arrows pointing up, down, left, and right.

The bridge lies between sheer rock walls guarding a majestic pool just below a steep waterfall. If there are fish anywhere in this system, it should be here. We should see them from the bridge. We don't see anything. But when it comes to steelhead, Mikey is a gamer. He gears up and negotiates a barely-there goat trail, hug-slides the canyon wall's warm rock, and boulder hops until he's descended the five hundred feet to the pool.

It doesn't take Mikey long to connect with a fish, but it's a small trout, not the steelhead he was targeting. While he casts, it's impossible to ignore just how loud the quiet here is. From below, the river whooshes, while above, the breeze hums and hisses through the green canopy.

Just a few miles downstream from this bridge is a sacred place known as Katimin, the Karuk's "center of the universe" and the site of an ancient Tribal village. Gold miners burned the community to the ground in 1852, and colonizers torched it again in 1883. By the 1950s, the government owned it. They sold four acres to a man who built a fishing lodge—forcing the Karuk to perform traditional renewal and salmon ceremonies off the property.

As a side-hustle, the lodge owner raised marijuana. Busted in 1993, he forfeited the land to the feds, who put it up for sale. After a year of negotiations, the government agreed to return the site to the Karuk. Not a progressive land-return policy, but something, I guess.

The river grows in power and volume as we track it west and north. Just four miles from where the river empties into the Pacific Ocean, the town of Klamath, California, doesn't have the battered look or the scattered State of Jefferson flags of upriver. Instead, there's a newish casino/hotel and the old-school "Trees of Mystery" attraction, where it costs $25 to walk among giant redwoods. But the town's real prestige comes from being the Yurok headquarters. The largest Tribe in California, the Yurok have never been forcefully removed from their land. Yes, it's been stolen, claimed, mined, dammed, and clear-cut, but today, the Yurok walk the same territory and paddle the same river their ancestors did. It is an immense point of pride.

Pre-contact, the Yurok people spread upriver and along the coast, populating more than seventy known villages. Change—monstrous change—was coming. Spanish colonizers Don Bruno de Heceta and Juan Francisco de la Bodega y Quadra anchored off Trinidad Head in June 1775. The invaders planted a cross and read the Requerimiento, a possession ceremony they claimed established their dominion over the land, and warned Native people they were now required to accept Christianity or face the consequences.

The Spanish initiated a wave of invaders hungry for plunder, land, pelts, fish, and timber. The gold rush flung the Yurok into deeper chaos. With the miners came pollution (rather than a romantic American interlude, the gold rush was one of the most devastating ecological events in world history), exploitation, land theft, and cultural and physical genocide. A grim paragraph in the Preamble of the Yurok Tribe Constitution illustrates the oppression:

> Our social and ecological balance, thousands and thousands of years old, was shattered by the invasion of the non-Indians. We lost three-fourths or more of our people through unprovoked massacres by vigilantes and the intrusion of fatal European diseases. The introduction of alcohol weakened our social structure, as did the forced removal of our children to government boarding schools, where many were beaten, punished for speaking their language, and denied the right to practice their cultural heritage. After gold miners swarmed over our land, we agreed to sign a 'Treaty of Peace and Friendship' with representatives of the President of the United States in 1851, but the United States Senate failed to ratify the treaty. Then in 1855, the United States

ordered us to be confined on the Klamath River Reserve, created by Executive Order . . . within our own territory.

Not content with confining the Yurok to a sliver of their ancestral lands, Congress passed the General Allotment Act of 1887, also known as the Dawes Act. Arguing the reservation had been abandoned, the Dawes Act gave small parcels of land to individual Yuroks. It offered the "surplus" to homesteaders. It was land theft on a massive scale, opening the door to widespread logging, mining, habitat destruction, and declining wildlife populations. It was also the first sign that something elemental to the Yurok way of life—the salmon—could be taken from them.

In yet another devastating blow, in the mid-1930s the State of California declared traditional fishing by Yurok people illegal. It took another fifty years and almost constant legal and even physical battles for those rights to be reaffirmed.

"When they put the dams in, it cut the river in half," says Barry McCovey Jr. For more than twenty years, he's been senior fisheries biologist for the Yurok Tribal Fisheries program. Barry speaks in long paragraphs about complicated things like genetics, salmon returns, and escapement. It can be challenging to keep up, especially when seals chase salmon in the bay behind him. "Basically, it destroyed the ecosystem," he says. "We see these dams as a monument to colonialism. This was about destroying people and culture for profit. We have ceremonies that require people to pray in the river. You can't pray if you can't even go into the river because it's toxic. If your dog drinks that toxic algae, your dog will die." He's referencing the algae blooms that accumulate behind Iron Gate Dam. In the summer, these blooms are released into the Klamath, coating the river bottom and banks with green slime. "We want to fix things," he continues. "We want to restore habitat, and we want to eat more healthy salmon. Costco chicken ain't cutting it. But it's not just for the Tribes. It will benefit everyone."

I ask him about the dam's defenders—the upriver folks who fiercely cling to the dams—and their concerns about irrigation, flood control, and electricity. How do you convince them that dam removal could ever be a good idea? "It's just misinformation," he says. "Everything we have in this watershed evolved in this flow regime. If you feel dam removal will hurt fishing opportunities, speak to a scientist. There are volumes about how dam removal can help fisheries. Don't rely on Facebook. Look at the research."

The question that everyone wants to have addressed by scientists like Barry is, what happens next? We've seen what the dam removal on Washington's Elwha River has done. Pacific salmon and steelhead were blocked from upstream spawning grounds on that river for nearly one hundred years. Steelhead populations tumbled to the point of near extinction. Following the breaching of the river's dams, summer-run steelhead came roaring back.

"Rivers are resilient. Fish are resilient," Barry says. "Our fish runs are depressed. There's no doubting that. As a scientist, I'm seeing increased disease exacerbated by dams and climate change. The dams warm up the river, and we see the toxic algae, which is quite literally killing fish—the dams are killing fish. There's no doubting that it could start to turn around, but we need to be patient. It took a very long time to fuck this up, but things will get better."

Then another obvious question. What happens, I ask, if the dams do come down? Will it be a celebration? Will it be bittersweet? He looks across the estuary. A few hundred yards away, the Klamath is becoming the Pacific. The sound of gulls and pounding surf mixes with the wind. "It's been a long time," he says. "People have dedicated their careers, their lives . . . people have died in the attempt to remove those dams. It's certainly going to be a victory. I can see it being very emotional. It's a huge milestone. As Yurok, restoring balance and fish is something we're born with. I was born with this weight on my shoulders. I was born to do this, but we also understand we'll always be fighting for this river."

I tell him about the rumors circulating for the last few days—that there's been a tentative agreement reached to finally bring down the dams. He smiles briefly and scans the estuary. "We've been near the finish line before," he says slowly. "I don't know how I'm going to feel. I haven't allowed myself to be there yet. When I see those excavators, I'll let you know."

⎯⎯⎯⎯⎯⎯

Pergish Carlson is quiet. Not standoffish quiet, but warm quiet. The sort of quiet that, when he begins a story, you lean in. "I know people more by their boat," he says, "than by their name." He laughs, slides his river sled off the trailer and into the waters of the lower Klamath. We are just three miles from the Pacific Ocean. The Klamath has settled into something languid and easy-going, far from the bustling waters below Iron Gate.

Our creation story begins here," says Pergish, gesturing to the water. "This is where my people come from. This is where my ancestors are buried." He points to a hillside across the river from a clearcut owned by a timber company. "My grandfather is buried just up there."

The Yurok have lived on this river for generation upon generation—thousands of years. The redwoods that line the bank have seen centuries of the river. Pergish himself has plied these waters for more than four decades. The four- and five-year-old steelhead we fish for have been here, in a practical sense, forever. The trees, the people, the fish, the river all describe time in humbling magnitude. It is time with a capital "T." It is a privilege for someone like me to fish Yurok land. The abundance. The fragility. The sense of spirit. The sense of time is palpable, like something we have put on—a formal frock of reverence.

We float down the river. It's quiet, and we are entirely alone. As upriver, the steelhead are nowhere to be found this early in the season. Instead, we amuse ourselves with "half-pounders"—juvenile steelhead that return to the river after less than a year at sea. They are feisty and readily smack a swung fly at the end of a decent cast.

While the rest of the crew engage the half-pounders, I walk with Pergish down a broad gravel bar. At every bend, every riffle, there's a connection. He points out an old Tribal village location, and then, across the river, another.

"Anywhere a creek comes in," he says, "there was a village. Ten or twelve structures and families per village. And they were made of wood," he chuckles. "We left no carbon footprint."

I look up into the trees and try to imagine life on this river. Pergish obliges my imagination, telling me about the many ways Yurok would harvest salmon. "We'd gather white stones and place them together on the bottom of the river. When they swam over the stones, we'd spear them." As we walk, he explains how the Yurok pioneered controlled burning to suppress wildfires, but also to safeguard the salmon. "When the river got hot, we would do burns. The smoke would create an inversion layer that would cool the river by three or four degrees allowing the fish to come up."

I ask how it feels to float this river and walk across these gravel bars in the shadows of so much history so close to the bone. "In the quiet times when I'm guiding, I'll think about that," he says. "It's something not many people can have . . . can understand. I feel lucky. I feel a real privilege."

We drift closer to where the river's journey ends, and the salmon's and steelhead's begin. I ask Pergish about the dams, the river, what could be. He grins like he's in on a secret. "It's a moral victory for us," he says. "We were promised so much with those dams, and when they came in, it was the end of everything. We battled for this river, and we won that battle. For thousands of years, we have never been defeated here." He pauses and a smile creeps across his face. "I had them all on my boat," he says, "all the big guys from PacifiCorp. I had fished them all day, and at the end, one of them said to me, 'I can't wait to come and fish with you again.' I told him, 'No. You can't fish with me until those dams start coming down. When that happens, then I'll take you fishing.' That was the last thing I said to him."

I meet Amy Bowers Cordalis in a small park overlooking Houda Point Beach and the magnificent stack rock formations standing sentinel in the Pacific. We are only a short distance from Trinidad Head, site of the Spanish landing. "This is still Yurok country," she tells me.

Amy is the Yurok's general counsel, a position equivalent to a state's attorney general. She is self-assured, with a mind always two questions ahead and a surprising, boisterous laugh. She speaks with her hands, answering my questions, while drawing arcs in the air to illustrate her points. She speaks at length about climate and racial justice on the Klamath and about how critical reconnecting the river is to her people. I ask her if the rumors are true—if her Tribe is about to make history. Her laugh jumps into the wind, "Yes!"

Rivers are patient things. Constructed in 1925, Copco #2 blocked the Klamath for ninety-eight years. Its last day was November 1, 2023. The smallest of the river's dams, it was used only for diverting the river into tunnels and pipelines. When it came down, there was no cathartic dynamite. Instead, the flows were controlled from above, and heavy equipment dismantled the dam, sealed the tunnels, and the job was done. Time-lapse videos make it seem simple.

It was impossible to get close to Iron Gate when its time came, so I scanned the web for video updates. Drawdown of the reservoirs began January 11, 2024. On that day, decades' worth of sediment—millions of cubic tons—began churning downstream, leaving vast mudscapes. Within a month, the Yurok were well into a remediation plan that included planting twenty billion native seeds and three hundred thousand trees and shrub plugs to restore the twenty thousand acres of land that had been underwater for so long.

It was all happening. The largest dam removal project in the history of the world was a reality. I kept thinking about my day at Iron Gate, its ugly buildings and sad picnic area. Mostly, I tried to imagine what it must have sounded like—what it must have felt like—when the dam's ever-droning hum finally surrendered to the whisper of the water.

These Waders Have Been Drinking

I will palm your lighter, spark a Winston, and then use it to open a bottle of beer from your cooler. I will take the bottle cap, and while you are running your mouth about some fatty you may or may not have roped, I will creep toward your waders. I know where they are—they're hanging from the roof racks on your rig. I will drop that bottle cap into those waders and then give them a shake to ensure that the cap falls to the lowest reaches of the boo- tie—all the way down into the toes. I will stifle an evil chuckle and rub my hands in delight. The deed has been done. Now we wait.

In the morning, you will be talking shit around the fire as you gear up. Have you forgotten the last time we fished together already? Of course you have. You will pull on your waders and, after everything has been tucked in and strapped down, you will feel that bottle cap. I will be secreted away, watching for that look on your face, the one that flashes first anger then submission.

You sputter, "Which one of you jerks capped me?" I will deny everything. I am prepared to make counteraccusations.

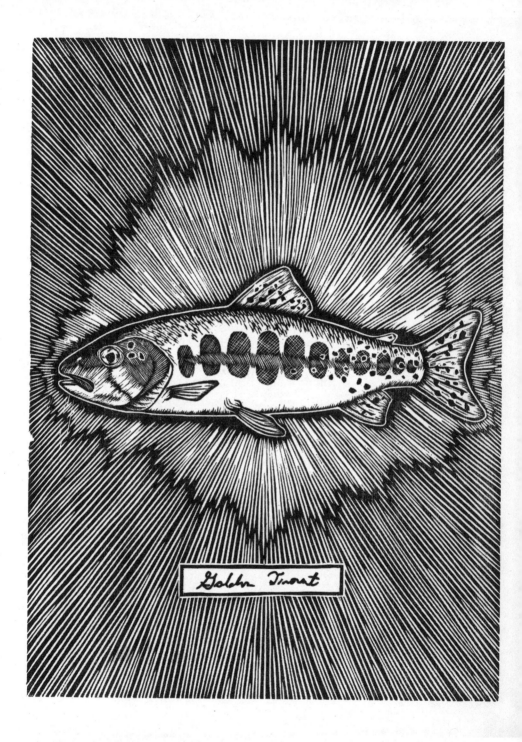

Golden Trout

11

GOLDEN TROUT
ARE A GOOD IDEA

Horses always seem like such a good idea, and this particular horse, Pockets, was everything we all love about horses: tall, stately, dignified, his big brown eyes radiating trust, steadfastness, and a gentleness in proportion to his size and power. Pockets even smelled good—that fecund mix of hay and clover, sweat and leather fittings. I rubbed his snout, told him he was a good boy, and wondered if his horse sense was alerting him to how utterly terrified of him I was.

Pockets was a thirteen-year-old mix of Morgan and quarter horse who had spent the first part of his career as an endurance racer. Horse people will tell you that Morgans are the all-American mount. Eager to please, they're known for their handsome profile, genial sense of humor, and charming manners no matter what task they are asked to perform. Quarter horses are a bit more stoic and down to business. Shorter than a Morgan, they're more muscular and constructed for long days on the trail cutting cows and doing other grueling cowboy stuff. Think of it this way: A Morgan is a golden retriever. A quarter horse is a border collie. It's a quality mix.

When I climbed up on Pockets, he turned his head to size me up. A rookie. A city slicker. A fancy-pants, freeloading scribbler decked out in free promo gear, a goofy ball cap, and hiking boots. He turned to a fat bunch of clover—his favorite. I white-knuckled the reins and tried to control my breathing.

Horses are a good idea if you know how to ride them—if you've spent time in the saddle, if you grew up around them and can read their moods, body language, and movements. When a horse snorts or nickers, does that mean something? Are there different types of whinnying? Is Pockets in a good mood or a bad mood? Is he going to bite me? If you don't know any of this stuff, horses can be intimidating, especially from the driver's seat.

Pockets didn't care about any of this. He assumed his place behind the feisty Dozer, an ever-farting dark-brown Arabian handled by our wrangler, Craig. At the back of our team were a pair of easygoing paints named Lightning and River, saddled by the photographer, Dan, and a fishing guide from the lodge, Kurt.

Soft-handed fly anglers, we were easy marks for the two cowboys. They didn't waste much time before they started digging in the spurs. Kurt tossed softball lines to Craig, who knocked 'em outta the park. "We had a little eight-year-old girl up on Pockets riding this route last week," Kurt said.

"Sure did," replied Craig. "Didn't complain but a one time. Caught a mess a trout, too."

"Yup, if I do recall. . . . "

"She really took to the horses."

"Yup. A natural."

We were a handful of miles outside Big Sky, Montana, and halfway up some foothills in the Spanish Peaks. We'd trucked up to a staging area, and after the cowboys finished tacking up and loading the gear onto the horses, the hooves were on the trail en route to Deer Lake, a high-alpine tarn said to hold a good population of grayling. This had the makings of not just a good idea, but a great idea. This was adventure. This sounded epic—a bucket-list trip in a wild and gorgeous place. I fidgeted around attempting to get comfortable in the saddle, and settled in.

An hour up the route and into the mountains, everything—knees, back, hips—started to ache. Maybe I'm a bit old for riding horses up steep wilderness trails. Maybe I'm weak. Maybe I'm a coddled suburbanite, but my legs were killing me, my calves were screaming in pain, and my ass was getting chapped. Pockets, however, was undeterred. He trudged ever upward into the thinning air, ignoring the staggering views and the mama moose and her calf, only interested in brief stops to munch another patch of clover or take long drinks from the tumbling little stream always in earshot. The cowboys—rugged, handsome, and bowlegged—spit chaw and announced that we were surely making good time. No. We were not. That was a lie. Time had stopped.

Lake-dwelling grayling are native in only two Montana locations, and Deer Lake is not one of them. Regardless, grayling have established a foothold and have a naturally reproducing population thanks to an outlet stream that allows them to spawn. While alpine lakes in the Spanish Peaks are hard to get to, these exotic trout cousins are not a secret. In 1959, the outdoors editor of the *Chicago Tribune*, Tom McNally, made this same trip to find these same fish. The big difference was that McNally didn't have a horse trailer to haul his team halfway up the mountains, so he had to ride eight more miles up and eight more miles down—twenty miles each way. In his report, he doesn't complain about sore knees and a chafed ass. He probably wasn't even afraid of the horses. He lays down some rapturous lines describing the scenery, and the fishing, of course, was lights out. He must have fallen in love with the place because when he retired several years later, he picked up his life in Chicago and set it back down again on the other side of these mountains, in Ennis, beside the Madison River.

We arrived at the lake after twelve miles and three excruciating hours in the saddle. Even if you are reclined in a comfortable leather seat sipping a latte in business class, three hours is a long time to be sitting. I dismounted to find that I could hardly stand. I hobbled around a bit, trying to stretch and loosen everything. I drank some water and began to dig through my gear, looking for the three-weight I wanted to string up. I'd packed two rods, two reels, three fly boxes, four spools, nippers, pliers, and a bunch of other stuff onto Pockets's broad back. I hadn't packed a single beer or even one tiny aspirin. Dumb.

It was sunshiny, a few clouds skittered, and a slight wind carried a suggestion of chill. The air was thin. It was difficult to focus—the setting, the exertion, the prospect of grayling swimming just a few feet away. I put my head down, concentrated on the fly box in front of me, and finally settled on a small black-and-maroon sparkle bugger—my favorite for high-altitude lakes.

Deer Lake sits in a glacial cirque more than nine thousand feet above sea level. It is surrounded by pines and crisscrossed by game trails. Toward one end of the lake is a vast talus field of bus-sized granite chunks painted with huge quartz streaks running through them like gleaming white graffiti. The lake was dimpled with fish rising here and there, and I scrambled over to one of those wide, flat granite slabs that allowed plenty of room for a back cast.

Regardless of the suffering needed to reach them, alpine lakes are always worth the effort. The first glimpse of them through the trees or from the trail is always heart-jumping. The water is clear as the sky, and the sky smells just like the trees hugging the lake. It's thrilling to think something so beautiful is secreted away and that you have found it. Below your feet is a planet of eight billion souls, and you and Pockets are the only ones blessed with a ticket to this wild, rare, and beautiful theater.

Across the water, Dan the photographer was setting up a staged shot. Kurt had climbed aboard Lightning and trotted him over to the lake. Dan handed him a fly rod. Kurt clicked his tongue and prodded Lightning with his heels to get him into position. They wanted that perfect postcard picture—a cowboy lassoing a trout from atop his trusty steed. First, however, they'd need to land that fly in the water, and then they'd need a trout to cooperate.

Kurt unhooked his fly and began to peel out fly line as Dan quickly crouched low to frame the scene while keeping Lightning in profile. The first cast never even got wet—the hungry branches of a Douglas-fir snatched the fly from the air. My laughter echoed off the granite, was captured in the natural amphitheater, and rolled across the water. The horses nickered.

I sent my first cast out to the middle of the lake, allowed the bugger to sink for a count of five, and slowly began to strip the line in. The water was so clear I could see the fly performing its clumsy, underwater blunder-swim from fifty feet away. So could a couple of grayling. They turned and accelerated, racing to be first to the fly. As usual, the little guy won.

As I gently pulled him closer, that iconic dorsal lit up with iridescent blue splotches as bright and alive as the sky. As the blue radiated toward the edge of the fin, it burst into a fiery orange border. The pectoral, pelvic, and anal fins were streaked with neon pink and glowing lavender. Grayling are so beautiful that it requires a moment to take them all in—to realize that this unlikely explosion of color exists in your hands as a pure and fragile thing that also happens to be quivering with life. They are stunning because they are real, living beings you can touch for a perfect, shivering moment, not some pixelated psychedelic fractal composed of ones and zeros.

Aside from impressive markings, a mountain grayling looks and fights like a whitefish. Yeah, this is a little disappointing, but so what? You cannot have everything. It's a lesson: Set reasonable expectations. Do not let your next, inevitable desires sabotage your real, present moment.

The fishing was not difficult. If you could find a clear place to cast and a grayling was within twenty-five yards of your fly, the fish would prick up his ears, swim on over, and take a bite. As I walked along the lakeside trail, the grayling were easy to spot, cruising the drop-offs, shoals, and ledges. They did not spook. They'd investigate a pebble tossed into the lake. They'd fight each other for the privilege of eating the bugger. It was easy, and every grayling taken was an opportunity to greedily ogle these fish.

Where did these colors come from? How did they get so resplendent? What's the purpose of that outsized dorsal? Every grayling, a fish Lewis and Clark dully called "a new kind of white or silvery trout," was a wonder. After release, the fish would not dart off, instead taking a few moments to find its bearings, regain some dignity, and flare those impossible colors—as if to see if the magical spots and streaks were still intact. Only then were they willing to fold those fins and casually swim toward deeper water. It was a remarkable, stately exit.

I finished rock-hopping, bouldering, and fishing around the lake and returned to our small basecamp. The cowboys were not cowboying. The photographer was not photographing. Everyone was too busy catching fish. I gave Pockets the apple from my lunch and stared at this impossible scene for a while, and then it was time to saddle up and suffer-trot another two-and-a-half hours back to the trailhead.

By the time we made it back down, I was beaten. Everything that hurt on the way up hurt twice as badly on the way down, and a substantial patch of skin had been removed from my ass. It sounds funny until it happens to you.

The lodge was called Lone Mountain Ranch. It was fancy. It even had its own saloon. I hobbled in. Other guests lounged at tables sipping cocktails while guides and wranglers held up the bar. I ordered a shot of local whisky and a pint, also local. The guides and cowboys were polite enough not to point and laugh.

Before too long, Craig and Kurt wandered in to join me for refreshments. The chef stopped by to announce that the bison steaks were fantastic and to solicit a fishing report. The bartender (bless his soul) came by with more beers to get a fishing report. Even the kid cleaning the stables clomped in to see if the grayling had been eating.

Outside the bar, children were playing in the twilight. Horses whinnied and snorted in the field next door, and the sound carried across some horseshoe pits. A young woman carried a yoga mat while a a man with a moustache and cowboy hat tuned a vintage Martin acoustic guitar on the bar's front stoop.

———

Archaeologists place hunter-gatherers from the Folsom culture in this area as far back as nine thousand years ago. To the Shoshone, this area of the Upper

Gallatin River was known as Cut-tuh-o'-gwa, or "Swift Water." The Shoshone called themselves Tukudika—the "meat eaters"—and that meat was bison. Their territory, also inhabited by Blackfeet, Sioux, and Crow, was a major buffalo-hunting tract that stretched from the Upper Snake River across the Gallatin Range and into the Upper Yellowstone.

In 1805, Lewis and Clark's Corps of Discovery—a band of forty-one men, mostly United States soldiers, one Shoshone woman, and one very large dog—straggled out of the mountains to the east, traveling westward. The Corps then returned this way the following year, this time headed back home to their own country. In their wake, trappers the likes of Jim Bridger, Jedediah Smith, and Joe Meek showed up hungry for pelts. They were followed by insatiable, lawless gold prospectors and, finally, the ferociously piggish Northern Pacific Railway. Montana became a United States territory in 1864. Not long after, the federal government established a cornerstone near present-day Willow Creek from which migrants mapped, surveyed, and claimed the entire Montana territory. By the time Teddy Roosevelt paid a visit in 1888, the West was closing fast and hard on the Shoshones and other Native American Tribes. Diseases, racist wars, crooked treaties, and other scheming conspired to decimate the Tribes, paving the way for Manifest Destiny. It was called progress. It was genocide.

In 1906, the Forest Homestead Act became law. This allowed citizens to claim agricultural land within national forests provided they occupy the claim for five years, cultivate the land, and construct a house and an outbuilding. There was a $10 filing fee. The land was $2.50 an acre—$85 in today's money.

In 1915, Clarence Lytle made his way to Gallatin County and established his 160-acre claim. Lytle put up a few cabins, cut some trails, and established his fence lines. He ran his homestead as a cattle and horse ranch, and did some hay cutting on the side. By 1926, Lytle, a bachelor, was finished with the hard work of ranching. He sold his stake to J. Fred Butler. It proved to be a good investment. Lytle was able to fetch $50 per acre from the wealthy paper-mill tycoon, netting a handsome profit of $7,600—close to $140,000 today.

Butler, aided by his daughter and son-in-law, Florence and Don Kilbourne, got right to work. He aimed to build the finest, most opulent ranch in Montana for his family and guests. He began clearing trees and erecting buildings. By 1927, Butler had purchased eleven more sections around the ranch and built eleven structures, as well as walking paths and a network of horse trails, spending an astounding $110,000 on his pet project. All the cabins had sod roofs on which Butler's wife, Lille, planted wildflowers. The linens inside the cabins matched the flowers on the roof. All the furniture was handmade and, in her spare time, Florence—the only child of a multimillionaire—snatched up a priceless trove of Native American artifacts to decorate the cabins. The pulls on the window shades were arrowheads. Navajo rugs were spread across the floors. Indian beadwork adorned the walls.

Butler passed away in the early 1930s; his survivors, stung by the Depression, decided to open the newly minted B-K Ranch to visitors. Their timing couldn't have been better. America had caught Western fever, and, aided by the automobile, visitors to Yellowstone National Park went from 18,000 in 1910 to 260,000 annually by 1930. The "dude ranch" was all the rage, and B-K was among the finest, offering camp trips, rodeos, horseback riding, cookouts, fishing, and every manner of Western entertainment.

The ranch has changed hands several times since the 1930s, but not much else has changed besides the name. Being so emblematic of a time and place, Lone Mountain Ranch was placed on the National Register of Historic Places in 2006.

It's a conflicted history, to be sure. I was on Indian land but sleeping in a plush cabin built by a usurping timber baron. I was riding ancient trails to explore the finest real estate in the world—stolen lakes, mountains, and streams. I was about to order a bison steak.

Besides the overt displays of nostalgia, the only Native culture in sight at the lodge consisted of the ghostly images in the black-and-white photos on the wall and the handful of archeological objects shown off in picture frames or under glass. If these scenes made me uneasy, I could only wonder how they affected the descendants of the Tukudika.

Morning always comes early for fishing guides, wranglers, and cowboys. It came crashing down like an avalanche on me. The effects of the horseback ride only got worse overnight. Now, the thought of humping a backpack past nine thousand feet to cast to fish that may or may not have even been there was no comfort. Only one thing got me out of bed: golden trout.

I'd never caught a golden trout but have cataloged the adjectives spellbound writers have used to describe them: *magical, magnificent, gorgeous, stunning, beautiful, exquisite. Hands down the most gorgeous fish that swims.* I ate three Advil, gulped some coffee, and bucked up. This was, after all, a bucket-list fish.

A mountain hike always seems like a good idea. Peace. Quiet. Fresh air. Exercise. The smell of the lodgepoles. The light glinting through the canopy. This hike was to take an hour and a half (straight up, both ways) on a trail unimaginatively named the Golden Trout Trail. The day was impossibly kind, with a warming sun that painted the ridges and pastures with an ever-sharpening light. Our guide, Jake, was an energetic twenty-something fish bum who already had a few seasons under his belt. He didn't walk; he bounded.

A mountain hike always seems like a good idea until the boots hit the ground, then thoughts of wildflowers, sprouting morels, and scenic views quickly give way to tight muscles, burning lungs, and thoughts concerning one's overall cardiovascular health. Jake scampered up the hill. Photographer Dan and I decided we were in no goddamn hurry and that attempting to keep up with Jake was a loser's game. We took our sweet time.

Golden Trout Lake was as hopelessly beautiful as Deer Lake. Upon casting eyes on a mountain lake, I always wonder, "How in the hell did this get here?" They always seem to appear out of nowhere, the entirety of the thing revealing itself after cresting one last ridge, as if to shout, "Surprise!" The next surprise is water so clear that it's easy to think that the fish aren't swimming, they are floating in the air.

We rigged up quickly and got to the business. There were some splashy rises out in the middle of the lake, well beyond casting range, but trout were at least here, they were allegedly golden trout, and by God, I was going to catch one or die trying.

I pulled the sparkle bugger off my hat—the same sparkle bugger that had shown no mercy to the grayling just the day before—and tied it on. I walked up the shore and found a fine-looking rock point, tottered out, and began to toss casts. Nothing. Nothing and more nothing. I was throwing bombs and inching the fly back as seductively as possible, but the goldens didn't care. They weren't having it. The wind began to pick up, and I considered the notion that a slight breeze at nine thousand feet could turn into gusts in a matter of moments. Gusts tend to ruin fishing trips. But then, something extraordinary happened: the wind, for once, became our friend.

In his book *Fly Fishing the Mountain Lakes*, Gary LaFontaine talks about anabatic winds—breezes created by warm air rushing up steep slopes. These are the winds that paragliders and raptors find so useful, but now it was our turn to use them. LaFontaine explains that anabatic winds dislodge all manner of bugs as they surge up the slope—beetles and ants especially. I took a wholly uneducated, unscientific guess and decided the reason goldens were now rising at the downwind side of the lake was because those bugs were landing there after a free ride up the mountain. I scrambled off the point, rigged a dry line and a flying ant pattern, and walked to the end of the lake.

Golden trout are only native to the Kern River drainage in California's Sierra Nevada range. Closely related to rainbow trout, goldens consist of three sub-species: the South Fork Kern, the Golden Trout Creek, and the Little Kern River golden trout. These fish typically live in tiny streams and never get much bigger than the palm of your hand. Tiny or not, they are still trout and the legend goes that in 1876, a timber-mill operator named Colonel Sherman Stevens wanted to catch some. Stevens and his brother managed to snatch thirteen golden trout from Mulkey Creek, a tributary of the South Fork of the Kern River. According to legend, Stevens stashed the still-living trout in a large pot and hiked four miles to the site of his sawmill, located on the banks of Cottonwood Creek. The goldens took in the creek, and, within no time, thanks to his sturdy boots and a strident belief in bucket biology, the colonel had his very own golden-trout stream.

Thanks to even more bucket biology, fish from Cottonwood eventually made their way into the area's mountain lakes. By the early 1900s, they were well known for their fine fishing and unusually handsome fish. They were so popular, in fact, that golden-trout eggs soon became a hot item. And even before a spawning station was set up at Cottonwood Lake to produce golden-trout eggs in 1917, batches harvested from traps in the lake were making their way to lakes across the West. A shipment of six hundred of these eggs made it to Montana and, eventually, Golden Trout Lake.

Montana importing trout eggs seems like taking sand to the beach, but these were lucky eggs. Golden Trout Lake is fine, unspoiled habitat. There is a spawning tributary. There is plenty of food. It's sufficiently deep and it is far, far from humans.

The trail skirting the lake was easy traveling, but I kept an eye out for Rocky Mountain high-alpine rattlers, marmots, and wild goats. You just never know. The fish were splashing regularly, and I could see Jake and Dan making their way over to my spot. I felt myself rushing to do everything at once—walk to the new casting area, determine where to cast, and worry about the bug selection, about the fish, about Dan and Jake walking over to steal my golden. It was a fever.

The first fish ate the ant following a mediocre cast and a mediocre drift, but there is no such thing as style points in fishing. I sucked in the thin air as I fought the fish back to the bank. What if it wasn't a golden? What if it was a cutthroat or a brookie? Could it be possible to be disappointed in any fish caught in a gorgeous Montana lake at nine thousand feet? Yes. Absolutely yes. This is a horrible thought, but there it is, the truth.

Nothing is remarkable about the fight in a golden trout. They could be better leapers. They could be faster and more powerful. They do not get very big.

Catching a golden trout is like catching any other trout in a mountain lake—it is a victory, yes, and there is a moment of almost being overwhelmed: the scenery, the impossibility of it, the pure, gorgeous luck.

That all happened—all those feelings—as I reeled. And then I saw a golden trout for the first time. The fish spun through the crystal-clear water, pulling against the line, fins flared, revealing something like the aurora borealis in the water. The colors—brassy copper struck through with a blood-red lateral line— were not just vivid; they were as alive as anything I'd ever seen—colors exploding into my brain.

I reached down to unhook her. She was remarkably cold—I expected her to radiate some kind of heat. Under her chin and extending down to the tail was a deep, deep crimson. Her flanks were painted with purple-thumbprint parr marks. Her tail was tattooed with indigo spots. Her fins were outlined in crisp white lines. She was remarkable. The most beautiful trout I'd ever held.

I blinked and wondered just how long I could hold her. Five seconds? Ten? She was about ten inches. A big golden, but I couldn't feel her weight. Why? Too much was going on with my other senses. I lowered her into the water. She paused, inhaled, and swam slowly away as a camera clicked and whirred behind me. I hadn't noticed Dan and Jake crouched next to me, whispering about how gorgeous that fish was, as if we were in some holy place where speaking out loud would be considered disrespectful.

I stood up and shook hands with the fellas, and then I think I hollered something, the sound bouncing around the cirque. I found a massive slab of granite. It had been warmed by the sun. I had a seat. There was nothing else I wanted to do.

After calming down a bit, I started fishing again. After all, the goldens were rising everywhere, snapping up the flying ants the anabatic winds had served up. We fished for another couple of hours until the feed turned off. It was deeply satisfying to look back at the lake as we shouldered packs and pointed our feet down the trail.

It was a different scene back at the ranch. Yeah, I was still sore and my ass was still chapped, but I had caught a golden trout. I don't want to report that the beer at the bar tasted better, that I gulped down dinner like a starving man, or that my heart was somehow lighter because that sort of thing sounds so fake, but it happened.

After dinner, as a bluegrass band was galloping through a version of "I Saw the Light" up on the porch, I walked over to the stables. I wanted to see the horses again. I wanted to apologize to them for all my bitching and moaning. I wanted to make peace with old Pockets and say thank you. It seemed like a good idea.

Tap the Brakes

When you first start fly fishing, no one tells you that committing to "the quiet sport" is also committing to the road—highways, rest stops, fast food, all of it. It's ironic that for an out-in-nature sport built on foot power—wading, hiking, scrambling, and exploring—one of fly fishing's constants is driving. Nine out of ten trips start and end with climbing into the truck, hoping the check-engine light has finally decided to turn itself off. It's true that fly fishing takes us to some of the most beautiful, pristine places in the world, but getting there involves a lot of staring out the window, looking at telephone poles, and counting the miles to the next bathroom break.

The drive from Seattle to southwest Montana may not look long on a map, but three hours outside Puget Sound, you've only just penetrated the formless scablands and arid desert steppe of eastern Washington. There are still six hours until Missoula. It's serious time in the saddle. Sports radio will only get you so far, and the blowhards shouting about politics and religion are a nonstarter. So, after the first bag of pork rinds has been downed, a few jokes told, and day jobs complained about, it's time for tunes.

We punctuate these long drives with music, filling in the blank spaces and empty stretches of highway. We use music to bide our time, soothe our anticipation, and celebrate our arrival. It's important, and when the journey is over, we connect the road and its rhythms with the trips, the people we share them with, and, of course, the fishing itself. One good thing about the gift of music, as Bob Marley wrote, is that "when it hits, you feel no pain." Still, for something so universally beloved, road music on a fly fishing trip can be a contentious issue.

I've certainly done my bit to fan these flames. I've subjected riding partners to everything from the Art Ensemble of Chicago's avant-jazz honk to Fela Kuti's propulsive Afro-funk to Hank Williams's three chords and the truth to blasts of punk, dubstep, drone, garage, jungle, and psych thrown in for added spice. But, like everyone, I'm both perpetrator and victim. I've also had to endure endless hours of music that makes time stand still. Music so bad and obvious that it became physically painful to hear. I'm not gonna name any names or tell you that your favorite band sucks because we tend to get really sensitive about matters of taste. No one wants to feel like a dork.

After more than a hundred thousand miles of fishing road trips, the truth I've excavated is that driving music functions as an unescapable karmic wheel. It is justice, and it grinds slowly. Suffering breeds suffering, and no one wants to suffer. So, in defiance of the whims of taste, there are ten protocols that, while not universally agreed upon by the unseen Universal Congress of Fly Fishing, are generally viewed as peacekeeping best practices.

THE TEN COMMANDMENTS OF ROAD MUSIC

1. **The Decider.** Driver's choice. Always and forever. This is the law of laws. The all-powerful edict that shall not be broken. The universal truth, upheld through the generations: touch that dial again, and I'll break your fingers.

2. **This Sucks.** Shotgun retains all rights to mock the driver's taste, age, and/or hipness based on music selection. There is no accounting for taste. We all like different things. But there are limits. If Commandment 1 confers absolute power to the Decider, Commandment 2 ensures a notion of artistic accountability.

3. **This Sucks in an Epic Way.** If there are three or more anglers in the same rig, a simple majority may, after four songs, offer the driver a formal objection to any music selection. (For procedural guidelines regarding lodging and raising "This Sucks in an Epic Way" objections, please see Commandment 1.)

4. **Peaceful Transfer of Power.** Decider may, at any time, relinquish music-picking responsibility to the angler riding shotgun. Before ceding duties, Decider may add unlimited conditions. Example: "Only country music released prior to 1972." "No rap-metal." "Go easy on the jam-band harmonica solos." Once relinquished, there are no "takebacks" of Decider privileges until the next rest stop/gas station, at which point Decider duties can revert to the Driver.

5. **Pump Up the Volume.** Teamwork makes the dream work. Cooperation and the ability to form consensus make for a good fishing buddy. With the driver's permission, the angler riding shotgun may adjust tone, balance, bass, treble, or volume. Otherwise, hands off.

6. **Sports.** Live sporting events are acceptable under any circumstances. Listening to the ball game while whizzing across the landscape is as close to the literal definition of "poetry in motion" as we will ever encounter. You have the rest of your life to listen to Slayer's *Reign in Blood*. The Mariners dropping their seventh game of a nine-game road swing only happens a couple times a year.

7. **Enough Already.** Avoid playing the same album/artist or playlist/mixtape/streaming station more than once a day. It's just good manners.

8. **The Hyphen Rule.** Avoid genres with more than three hyphens if traveling with an aged or musically conservative passenger. Examples: downtempo-post-dubstep or folk-punk-nerdcore. More a suggestion than an absolute commandment, the Hyphen Rule is a guidepost pointing us toward good behavior. The entire reason for the existence of the commandments is to aid in road-trip peace. We seek only good vibes for all.

9. **The Grateful Dead Rule.** While perfectly legal under Commandment 1, actively tormenting passengers with extremely long bouts of objectionable music is frowned upon and should be limited to forty-five minutes or one live version of "Drums/Space"—whichever is longer. Misunderstood by many, Commandment 9 is not a slight

to the San Francisco band formerly known as the Warlocks. The Dead are just fine. Having numerous fishing buddies who are highly committed to this outfit, I've listened to thousands of hours of Dead shows. I prefer their Americana/bluegrass-leaning stuff, personally. In fact, the groovy, back-porch vibe of Jerry's "Old and in the Way" strumming is downright lovely. So, whatever, hippie.

10. **No Self-Dealing**. Playing your own demo, last open-mic recording, or rehearsal is forbidden unless requested. It probably won't be requested.

12

LEGENDARY RIVERS
I DIDN'T FISH

Just before tea, about 3:30 in the afternoon, it's a balmy 39 degrees Fahrenheit and hailing—another splendid August afternoon in the Scottish Highlands. We've been driving since early morning. The singer is pouting, adamantly sticking to her vow of silence. The drummer is furious at the fiddle player for breathing too loudly. In turn, the fiddle player threatens the drummer with violence for allegedly filling in rows 7, 8, 9, 11, 16, and 25 on her crossword puzzle. The roadie/banjo player (me) wants to choke the life out of everyone in the minibus. We are hungry, thirsty, and tired, and no one knows the exact location of tonight's gig. At that moment, as we pass over another bustling, trout-packed stream etched into the hills near Dalwhinnie, I realize how grim my situation has become. How did I end up in the far-flung northern-UK wilds, probably lost, certainly hungover, and utterly devoid of any sort of angling implements?

More than a few pints were involved. There was the sexy-smart singer who looked like an angel and sounded like Loretta Lynn with her hair on fire. The all-gal band was shit-hot and could play both country and western. They needed a combination driver, soundman, roadie, instrument tech, T-shirt seller, tour manager, and part-time banjo picker for an absurdly unfeasible fifty-gigs-in-fifty-three-days Euro tour. Hey, no problema, baby. I'm your guy. Where do I sign up?

GLASGOW, SCOTLAND

Glasgow is ablaze. The national squad and their loyal fan mob have mustered for a home match at the Hampden Park football pitch—a World Cup qualifier. A "wee bit ay thee fitbaw" against some overmatched Eastern European team. Cops are squared up everywhere, eyes darting, heads on swivels. Sweaty, cheek-to-jowl, and tense—every bar is at capacity, and jittery punters in the white and blue of the national side pace the sidewalks huffing hand-rolled smokes. Gangs of men amuse themselves by chanting, singing, chasing fans of the opposing side through the streets, fighting them, and then setting dumpsters on fire. Smoke bombs are going off. Sirens. Chaos. There are still three hours to go before the first ball is booted.

The night's gig is in an ancient stone church a few blocks from the stadium. At sound check, the music echoes off the walls in a crazy, ping-pong confusion. A Gregorian chant or a string quartet may flutter to the heavens on gossamer wings in one of these old crypts, but try conjuring a coherent sound out of hillbilly harmonies, a couple of guitars, a fiddle, a banjo, and a lot of foot-stomping. It's a nightmare.

We make it through the gig. It's fine, and by "fine" I mean, "OK." They can't all be worthy of the Grand Ole Opry. There is a bright spot. For the encore, everything comes together as we buzzsaw through a cover of Dolly Parton's "Jolene." UK audiences love that one. Everyone loves that one. Outside, as we load gear into the minibus, the dumpster fires still rage. There is screaming, more sirens, more chaos. It's obvious the football match did not go as anticipated. We step into the confusion of a full-on riot. Red-faced men are running everywhere, throwing things and lighting more things on fire. We can't escape; there is no way out. The cops tell us to stay put. It is well into the early morning before we exit Glasgow. If you are in Scotland on a night the home team plays a crucial match, please remember there is no satellite navigation app to help you circumvent the outward display of grief and dis-appointment following a football dustup.

THE RIVER SPEY, SCOTLAND

We sleep in a parking lot and rise with the sun at 5 a.m. We have a long drive north to the next gig in the Highlands. Despite the misery, the ride is lovely—until I don't fish the River Spey.

Crushing, because from the motorway the Spey is a stunning-looking river. Soft green banks are home to lolling, well-groomed cattle. The sheep are fat and untroubled, and the hawks gliding overhead seem at peace. The river has a gentle, gurgling gait, languid bends, and an uncanny way of catching the light. And yeah, there are even tidy bits of ruined castle strewn perfectly here and there. It's a painting. It looks unreal. If Disney wanted to create an animatronic "Olde Scottish" salmon stream, this is what they'd come up with. However, if you're not fishing it, the Spey is dismal.

To make not fishing the Spey even more painful, the A95 travels along the river, offering peeks every few kilometers. It's akin to driving along I-90 in Montana, gazing upon the Clark Fork every five minutes. *There it is. There it is again. Have another peek? Look at that perfect run! Was that a fish rising?* My traveling companions, of course, do not give a toss that the Spey, along with the Dee, the Tay, and the Tweed, is one of the "Big Four" Scottish fly fishing rivers. They do not care that the Spey is home to its own style of fishing. They do not care that there is even a thing called a "Spey rod."

I attempt to impress upon them the gravity of the situation with a con-versation starter—"Ya know, the River Spey is known the world over for . . ." —only to suffer ironic hipster pity and cynical wisecracks.

It has been raining, hailing, and howling since we left sad, battle-torn Glasgow, and as the Spey gradually opens up into its regal Speylike size and shape, the sun pries itself from the clouds, exploding prismatic dew that shimmers the grass and tosses a spray of diamonds over the surface of the famous river like an image from some improbably perfect magazine story in which everybody catches fish, the shore lunch is delicious, and the dogs back at the lodge are all golden retrievers trained to fetch icy-cold beers.

We hustle right on by. We don't even slow down, honk the horn, or flash the lights in tribute. I feel ill. It's a sad welcome. Scotland, what have we done?

We also motor right by a few distilleries (Cardhu, Dalwhinnie) and some quaint-looking pubs offering strong ales. Horrible. Frustrating. Soul-crushing. But we have a gig to make. I console myself, as always, by thinking that given a day or two, my own gear, and the right flies, I could really do some damage on the Spey. Atlantic salmon? Pffft. Compared to steelhead on the Olympic Peninsula, Atlantic salmon are probably easy to catch.

Against hooting protest, I pull over and stop for all of forty-five seconds to snap a perfectly annoying shot of a perfect bridge over a perfect bend, stood sentry by a perfect little fishing shed on the perfect Spey. A perfect Scottish river I didn't fish.

DORBACK BURN, SCOTLAND

In Scotland, "burn" is the term for a creek, and please note that it's pronounced *bahh-err-ne*, just as in some areas of the United States, creek is pronounced *crick*. Despite our differences, we have a few things in common. Chief among them is the stubborn refusal of secretive anglers to speak in anything resembling a language that non-fishing civilians can understand.

Local color aside, the Scottish Highlands (or "Hee-lunds") remind me of parts of Wyoming. Both are jammed full of lovely bits of contented, meandering nothingness set back-to-back with strikingly singular chunks of Nature's best work. The significant difference between the two landscapes is that Scotland lacks the crushing heft of huge mountains as an ever-present background. The Scots, however, tend to get feisty if you refer to their hills as, well, hills. Some advice—let it slide. If they want to call a hill a mountain, so be it. You don't want to start haggling over some minor point with a Scotsman because he will never—ever—let it go. You cannot win.

Before a gig on the Isle of Islay (the one famous for delicious Scotch whisky), a punter wobbles up to our merch table, screws up his mug, and blurts, "Aye, ye know whae, laddie?"

"I dunno, dude—what?"

"In Sco-lund we invented coont-ra music. Aye, that is aye fer-certain fact, laddie!"

"That right, dude?"

"Aye, fookin' gospel, son!"

At this early juncture in our relationship, this fellow seems more than willing to go fist-to-cuffs defending his point. He is a wee squirt and pretty drunk, but dangerously aggressive and eager to drop the gloves if I do not offer a ringing endorsement of his statement.

Unfortunately, there is no way in hell I'm doing that. So, I do what I usually do in these tricky, "culturally sensitive" situations: I remove my cowboy hat, take a long, thoughtful ponder at the sweat ring around the brim, and offer a slow nod and grunt, signaling neither agreement nor disagreement.

It works. It always works. He nods his bean along with me, claps me on the back, and then carts over a steady brace of pints to the side of the stage the rest of the evening.

The drive to the night's gig is mercifully short and achingly beautiful. We are afforded a few, horribly brief glimpses of the horribly beautiful Dorback Burn, about a mile after passing yet another sign claiming that we have, indeed, migrated into "whisky country." I don't need the reminder.

The Dorback is a sweet little tumbler. It glides and bounces and rushes hither and yon. I'm sure a metric shit-ton of cute browns reside contentedly in its flow. I'd wager some big boys are skulking under those nice undercuts and overhanging grassy banks, but then again, how would I know? I ain't fishing it.

THE RIVER TAY AND THE RIVER EARN, SCOTLAND

Just outside the town of Pitlochry, we cross a big, fishy-looking river. Generally, there are no signs in Scotland telling you where the hell you are, where the hell you are going, or how long it's gonna take you to get there. Still, for some reason, there is a sign, and the sign reads "The River Tay."

Oh.

To make this bad situation worse, just as we cross the bridge, an angler is heading to the water with a Spey rod locked and loaded. He is pointed toward a vast, sweeping pool fed by a riffled waterfall. It looks perfect and horrific at the same time. We speed right on by.

According to the pamphlet from the Scottish tourist board that I'd picked up, the River Tay is "one of the best salmon rivers in the United Kingdom, and therefore the world." Reading it as a steelhead junkie from the Pacific Northwest, I chuckle indignantly and think, "Yeah, sure." But who knows? I refuse to believe it because this non-fishing expedition threatens to turn me incredibly bitter, and to accept that a river I crossed without fishing may be one of the finest salmon rivers on the planet is simply too close to self-flagellation.

To get to the night's gig in Crail, a village on the east coast, we must pass through St. Andrews, where a lot of serious golf is performed. You can tell St. Andrews is a golf town because the course is literally on the main drag, and people are sporting the most incredible slacks. It's all quaint, charming, and fertilized with a lot of money, but at least the golf course keeps these people off the rivers that I'm not fishing.

We drive through the rolling countryside practicing our four-part harmonies and, after awhile, pass over the River Earn. I only steal a quick glance and have nothing to report about this sweet little crick, for alas, there are only so many rivers that I can't fish in one day.

THE RIVER WYRE, ENGLAND

After a few gigs down in England, we head back north. Crossing the River Wyre, I finally break. Hot, frustrated tears dribble down my cheeks. I bury my head in a pile of tour T-shirts. The band, engaged in a rather heated Johnny Cash vs. Buck Owens vs. Merle Haggard debate, is oblivious to my blubberings.

Arriving at the gig in Leith—a gritty neighborhood in Edinburgh—I brace myself with copious amounts of the local refreshment. The gig is packed, sweaty, and raucous. The whole crowd sings along to "Jolene." Afterward, I sell seventeen T-shirts stained with my tears—a tour record. Not fishing Scotland? Sometimes a good cry can help.

THE RIVER TWEED, SCOTLAND/ENGLAND BORDER

The air conditioner gives up the ghost just in time for Scotland's annual week of summer. We are very dirty and very stinky, heading north to a gig in Montrose. My nerves are on edge, however, and as the driver, I make an executive decision to pull over—lo and behold!—right next to a river. I park under some tall, rustling willows on the English side of the Tweed, hop out, and hightail it down a path toward the water, camera in hand. I cross a gate, and only twenty-five yards from the river, I come up short. Ay! There it is, a sign that confirms my worst fears regarding fishing in the United Kingdom—all that permitting, private-water, upstream, dry-flies-only-on-days-ending-in-y business.

FISHING BY PERMIT ONLY!
BEAT NO. B.
2 RODS.

I cannot abide the notion of private fishing water. The thought that someone owns the river, the fish, or the water kickstarts my inner anarchist, compelling me to jump fences, deface signs, and pontificate on the internet. However, this is the first time I've confronted a sign marking the strangest of UK fishing regulations—a "fishing beat," a.k.a. a stretch of river on which the fishing rights are held by the landowner who owns the land adjacent.

In my not-fishing, agitated condition, this is an entirely new sort of outrage/affront/injustice, and I roll its sour taste around on my tongue. Fishing a beat is foreign to the constitution of an angler from the American West. We are built to ramble. We are inclined to load up a pack with cans of cheap beer and beef jerky and get the hell outta Dodge—away from the jerks fishing right next to the road or the boat launch. We love taking off into the outback for the mere fact that:

1. We can.
2. Well, just what the hell is around that bend?
3. We pride ourselves on an exceptionalism bred into our bones which dictates that the wild, the back forty, the untracked places *belong* to us. Fishing with the rabble seems a compromise, a cop-out—something for the very young, the very old, or the very lazy. Real anglers are not to be constrained—especially by something like a sign.

I'm hopped up and stomping the rest of the way to the water, high off the delicious self-righteousness of it all. And there she flows. The great River Tweed. So much tradition. So much of the very essence of our sport flows inches in front of me. I smell the history mixing with the tumble of the current, the grassy bank, and the trees spilling pollen. It is an impossibly scenic river—castles, old rowboats, a stone bridge. In the distance, two old dudes sit in a boat, rods in their hands, waiting. A fish jumps directly in front of me in a handsome, riffle-pocket-riffle stretch. *Cripes.*

What are those dudes doing sitting in the frog water? There are never fish in the frog water. Just what the hell are they thinking? I don't know. I never know. Yet every time I see a dude fishing the frog water I wonder, "What the hell are you thinking?"

The fish that jumps in front of me is, of course, nice and big. I am confident I could catch it if I were fishing the Tweed, which I am certainly not. I walk back up the bank, past that stupid, goddamn sign, and climb into the van.

THE RIVER TEST, ENGLAND

If you want to fish Thee Olde and Faymous Ryver Test, you must first pay the man—Albert Victor Nicholas Louis Francis Mountbatten, 1st Earl

Mountbatten of Burma. Though the Irish Republican Army assassinated Mountbatten while he was lobster fishing in 1979, the Test, without a doubt, remains his domain. This river is currently occupied by his descendant, Norton Louis Philip Knatchbull, 3rd Earl Mountbatten of Burma (second cousin to the king of England). His "associates" string razor wire and patrol the banks of the Test like Tony Soprano patrolled Jersey.

All this would be fine if the Test were just some middling English trickle, but alas, looking from the side of the road, behind the barbed wire and just out of the reach of the attack hounds, I see that Lord Mountbatten's river looks like a pretty great trout stream.

The Test is only about forty miles from start to finish, and lumbering brown trout jam its upper chalk-stream reaches. I ogle them as I stand on a stone bridge while trucks, taxis, and bikes whiz past. Upstream of the upscale, touristy village of Romsey, fish rise to tiny white mayflies even as a goofy black lab splashes and gallops in the water. The sad fact is the River Test is packed cheek-to-jowl with well-mannered trout. Even a non-angler can see big browns swimming around. Can't catch a fish here? League night. Cool shoes. White Russians. Strikes and spares.

Gaze along the riverside path and scope the quaint, bank-bound fishing huts. The history of the place is palpable—and so is the money. Let's say you're feeling flush, or an acute case of Anglophilia overtakes the senses and you simply must fish the Test. It's gonna cost. A beat (pfft!) on the Test—if you can get one (you can't)—costs a small fortune. So many fish guarded so tightly by so many wealthy royal dicknobs.

There are no dirtbag fishermen on the Test; there is no sleeping in the back of the pickup. Hanging around the parking lot, crushing beers, spitting dip, and cranking "Folsom Prison Blues" is unheard of. When was the last time these banks felt the toasting of a campfire, hosted a ring of tents, and silently nodded as half-true stories were told under a clouded moon? Call it "tradition" if you must. I think, Lordy, what a waste of a perfectly good piece of trout water.

RIVER AVON, ENGLAND

Upstream on the Avon, Shakespeare emptied his chamber pot, G. E. M. Skues refined nymph fishing, and Frank Sawyer invented the pheasant-tail nymph. For a fly angler, those are significant historical landmarks.

We arrive for the night's gig at a rather posh (at least for us) arts center in Bristol, overlooking the river. We look forward to art-center gigs—the pay is excellent, the dressing rooms are clean, the sound guy is competent, and they're usually even catered. No fish and chips tonight! No, ma'am. Tonight, we may even see a green vegetable!

This enormous venue includes two restaurants, two bars, four stages, a movie theater, and an entire wing of classrooms and studios. We're booked to play a stage with a capacity of two hundred. We see the line stretching around the block as soon as we hit the parking lot. There are easily two hundred people queued up already. Usually our fans only bother showing up after the streetlights are on, but this time the joint is jammed by four in the afternoon. I can make out cowboy hats, so surely these are our fans. But something else catches my eye.

As a touring band, you're open to anything and welcome anyone who pays their money and walks through the door, but the honest fact is, we just don't draw a lot of fans with portable oxygen packs and mobility walkers. Our demographic isn't—and there's only one way to say this—the elderly. But there they stood, hopeful, eager, high off the anticipation that only a quality, shit-kickin' country punk hootenanny can promise.

I grab my banjo and duck into the stage door and right into Dolly Parton's breasts. Only something isn't quite right. Dolly isn't right. Her breasts are different than I remember. When she says, "Hi! How're you?" I put her accent closer to South London than Tennessee. Then another Dolly Parton walks into the dressing room, stuffing her hair under an enormous blond wig. Everyone in the band—all of us—stands speechless. There are simply no words. None. I remove my cowboy hat and meditate upon that sweat ring, squinting and wishing I could summon the wherewithal to grunt meaningfully.

We have, it turns out, crossed paths with the Doll Girls, "Europe's Finest Dolly Parton Tribute." There are two Dolly Partons (old Dolly and young Dolly) along with a full band, a chorus, dancing, skits, and hilarity of every variety—all this for only £30—and you're home before those streetlights switch on.

The Doll Girls' merch table is forty-five feet long. It includes cheap cowboy hats embedded with flashing LED lights, bandanas, bobbleheads, posters, DVDs, and a bewildering, tasteless assortment of doodads decorated with the Confederate battle flag. Of course, it's easy to say this scene is hilarious—it is. But it is also exasperating. We've come all the way from Seattle to rip the lid off some gen-u-ine, cry-in-your-beer, pick-your-mama-up-from-jail-in-a-stolen-pickup, fist-fighting twang 'n stomp, and the Doll Girls show up with fake accents, lip-synching, cornpone gags, and racist memorabilia. At the door, fake Dolly outsells authentic us three to one.

After our sound check, I walk into the lobby and hear Dolly's crowd stomping along to "Jolene," a song I loved until that moment. "Jolene" is *our* Dolly song! I step out to seethe and take in River Avon. The breeze is cool, and I smell salt in the air. I see a few fish splashing way out near the estuary. Are they trout? Could they be salmon? Down below, a wooden boat moves and an anchor splashes. A younger guy stands up and peels line off his reel. He is in the frog water. I can't even watch.

We end the tour in mainland Europe, driving up and down the Netherlands and playing festivals and bar gigs in Germany, Belgium, and France. We even play a strange gig at a non-ironic cowboy bar in Luxembourg. Out of the blue one non-fishing morning, I realize not only is the tour almost over, but so is my fishing drought. Fifty gigs. Eight thousand miles. Not one river fished. Not one line cast. Not one trout grabbed up. Not a single salmon molested. That must be some sort of record. I'll be home in time for the end of trout season and the beginning of salmon. For steelhead. For my fish.

So, what did I learn? Well, lots, really, like when you're not fishing and being forced to watch other people fish, you have the opportunity to cultivate profound, sanity-saving patience. When you practice catch and release without ever—ever—catching a fish, you can become adept at a particular type of "letting go" that has absolutely nothing to do with trout, rivers, or fishing. Honestly, it's a pretty good skill to have. The road breeds all manner of toxic, toothed, wriggling aggravations. When you can let those moments slip back into the stream with the same generosity we afford trout, it makes the tour, the gig, and the music all the sweeter.

Steelhead as a Fragrance

Armpit, ash, ass, bacon, baked beans, Band-Aids, bar floor, basalt, BBQ, bear grease, beer, blood, bourbon, buffalo shit, campfire, cedar, chew, chicken, cigarettes, cigars, coffee, cold pizza, cold stars, cold water, cow shit, crotch, dirt, dog, dog breath, dog shit, Douglas-fir, dust, elk shit, fish hands, formaldehyde, fresh snow, fryer grease, garlic, gasoline, Gatorade, grease, hail, hops, hamburger, hot water, Jägermeister, jerky, meat, menthol, mold, mud, night air, orange juice, pastries, pillow, pinesap, pit toilet, propane, rain, river, river froth, river mist, river rock, river slime, sage, salami, scotch, skunk, sleet, snow, spit, stale beer, sweat, sweetgrass, tobacco, urinal mints, weed, wet wipes, whisky, wine, wool.

13

A STOLEN SUNDAY

For twenty-five years, "The Drinking Fisherman" has hung on a north-facing wall of my living room. The wall is painted mustard yellow and is home to my favorite angling art. Most of the pieces are the bold, starkly beautiful crimson-and-black figures of salmon rendered by Native artists of the Northwest. There is also a watercolor by James Prosek, a few impressionistic miniatures of trout painted in thick, gestural oils, and a piece of soft pine carved into a Salish representation of a salmon egg. "The Drinking Fisherman" stands in plain contrast to the splashes of color on the wall, as it is the only photograph in the modest collection.

"The Drinking Fisherman" is set in a basic wooden frame, but despite his no-frills home, he's provided countless moments of delight and wonder for me. Who is this person posing on the banks of a river dressed in thick wool breeches, high leather boots, and a silly little silk tie? He wears his hat tipped back for the camera, but even at that abrupt angle, it's easy to tell that the brim is broad and sturdy. It keeps the rain off the head and the sun out of the eyes. The hat is a bit grimy with accumulated luck, but it's still stylish, and he must think it makes him look sporting. It's not the hat for weddings and Sundays—it's a bit too battered for a special occasion—but on the river it works simply, and simply works.

Under a collared shirt, bunched up under his sleeves, the Drinking Fisherman wears what appears to be a thermal undershirt. Perhaps it's a full union suit, one he's been wearing all week, beer swipes and chewing tobacco smudges be damned. Regardless, some insulation up top is in order, as the icy current will flow right through those wool knickers.

Personally, I've never worn a tie while angling. I've never even considered it. It seems somehow . . . wrong. But a possible explanation is there before us, plain as the spring Sunday in the picture—the Drinking Fisherman is dodging church services for a more spiritual, one-on-one meetup with the maker.

His high leather boots are laced tight over a pair of thick woolen socks. The boots provide excellent ankle support, and the soles are likely studded with hobnails providing reliable traction, especially on slick rocks and boulders. Lastly, our man is wearing a split-willow creel. Buckled in, braced up, and ready to go, the Drinking Fisherman is ready to hit the water, from the sturdy boots to the crisply brimmed beak. He is young, well built, and stoked for a fine day chasing his Sunday supper.

To keep his future catch cool, an angler would usually pad his creel with river grasses—mint and watercress. But we have evidence that our angler stashed beers instead. That beer—cool and delicious, foaming with agitation from the hike-in—is meeting its purpose in the photograph. And how good it must have been, at that moment, on that Montana bank, bestride that trouty flow before a day on the water. Doesn't get any better.

"Ah! my beloved brother of the rod," wrote Francis Francis, the renowned English angling bard from the late 1800s, "do you know the taste of beer—of bitter beer—cooled in the flowing river? Take your bottle of beer, sink it deep, deep in the shady water, where the cooling springs and fishes are. Then, the day being very hot and bright, and the sun blazing on your devoted head, consider it a matter of duty to have to fish that long, wide stream. An hour or so of good hard hammering will bring you to the end of it, and then—let me ask you *avec impressement*—how about that beer? Is it cool? Is it refreshing? Does it gurgle, gurgle, and 'go down glug' as they say in Devonshire? Is it heavenly? Is it Paradise and all of Paris to boot? Ah! If you have never tasted beer under these or similar circumstances, you have, believe me, never tasted it at all."

And what of that heavenly beer our angler was knocking back? There's no label in the image, and the brew foams mightily. Was it a homebrew—boiled up on the kitchen hob just weeks earlier? Due to the often-uncontrollable carbonation levels, these jugs were notoriously volatile, apt to explode at any moment. All the more reason, I suppose, to pack two in that creel—just in case.

"Guzzle guzzle, go down glug. . . . "

Even though we are witnessing a moment of beery satisfaction, there is still anticipation left to savor in this photograph. It is an image loaded with possibility, high hopes, vigor, promise, and prospect. We are not just spectators; we are eager participants on that bank. We fidget and wait for the photo to be made, our own beer sweating in our hand, a new fly tied to a spider-thin leader, eager for the first trout to make that first mistake. A day, already so close to perfection, is just now about to get even better. The beer is not celebrating the end of a day; it's inaugurating its beginning.

———

When I found the photograph, the 4-x-5-inch glass negative from which this image is printed was owned by a soft-spoken man named Thomas Robinson. He sold prints of "The Drinking Angler" on his website and at flea markets, swap meets, and antique shows around his home in Portland, Oregon. Long a collector of vintage glass negatives, Robinson had once followed up on a lead concerning an extensive collection of glass-plate negatives owned by an elderly man from Missoula, Montana. After a short negotiation, a few boxes of the fragile negatives were purchased. In one of those boxes, Robinson uncovered our Drinking Fisherman. "Other than that," he says, "I just don't know too much about it."

Robinson believes the image dates from the early days of the twentieth century. "I'd guess around 1910 or 1920," he says. Perhaps the photo was taken in 1910, on an early lark upon the still-bright tracks of the Great Northern Railway to the just-established gates of President William "Big Chief" Taft's Glacier National Park. Or was it 1914, the year of the first great World War and the era of President Woodrow "the Professor" Wilson, who would lead the United States into that very conflagration in just a few years? Could it have been the summer of 1918, months before the hated Dries pushed Prohibition onto the backs of honest drinking fishermen and fisherwomen across the country?

Dries vs. Wets. How the nation must have heaved. How intensely the fate of its moral arc was debated. It must be noted, however, that Prohibition was never popular in Montana. In fact, Montana was far removed from the pious cries of the Dries, who, prodded by the powerful Anti-Saloon League and the Women's Christian Temperance Union, tended to be Methodists, Baptists, Presbyterians, Disciples, Congregationalists, Quakers, and Scandinavian Lutherans. Wets, primarily Episcopalians, German Lutherans, and Roman Catholics, tended to side with the more libertarian ethos of the rapidly changing West. This landscape had recently witnessed the no-holds-barred escapades of the likes of Doc Holliday, Liver-Eating Johnston, Boone Helm, Butch "Cassidy" Parker, and Harry "the Sundance Kid" Longabaugh. True to form, Montana was the first state to repeal the enforcement of the Eighteenth Amendment—Prohibition—in 1926. It took until 1933 for the Twenty-first Amendment, repealing Prohibition, to finally become the law of the land.

Truth be told, Prohibition never really had a chance in Montana, where the consensus was in concord with Will Rogers, who remarked that "Prohibition is better than no liquor at all." Butte, one of the most prosperous towns in the emerging West, had more than two hundred bars and three breweries before Prohibition. After Prohibition became the law, more than a hundred speakeasy establishments flourished, and the bathtub gin, the applejack, the corn, and moonshine flowed freely, thanks to moonshiners like John F. "Jack" Melia. Melia was more than just a moonshiner, though. He also happened to be the head of the squad appointed to enforce Prohibition—the fox literally guarding the henhouse.

The university in Missoula and the ag college out in Bozeman were thirsty, too. They sat happily downstream of this flow of kill devil, tiger spit, thunder 'n lightnin', and tanglefoot, and eagerly drank all they could swallow. But beer was the favorite lubrication in the Montana boomtowns now filling up with German and Irish miners.

There is little doubt that if our Drinking Fisherman did not procure his suds from the likes of Missoula's Garden City Brewery, there was always Butte Brewing, Tivoli, or the gigantic Centennial Brewing Company (1905 slogan: "A million glasses a day, someone must like it!").

Odds are, he's probably drinking beer that he—or someone he knew—brewed themselves. In the early days of the twentieth century, especially under the confines of Prohibition, homemade beer was a more straightforward proposition than it is today, and one not so concerned with hop pedigrees, carefully cultivated yeast strains, and organic malt blends. Homebrew was more about function than form. Early recipes are simple: a large can of hop-flavored malt syrup, a few scoops of granulated sugar, water, and a yeast cake. The mixture was covered with cheesecloth and left until the obvious signs of fermentation died. The beer was siphoned into another large container, more granulated sugar was added, and the beer was quickly bottled. Nothing fancy, but in ten days the beer was ready to drink. A talking-blues, recorded by South Carolinian Chris Bouchillon in 1926—and later covered by Woody Guthrie—paints the scene:

> Mother's in the kitchen, washing out the jugs.
> Sister's in the pantry, bottling the suds.
> Father's in the cellar, mixing up the hops.
> Johnny's on the porch, watching for the cops.

If the story begins with our angler's streamside answer to the Dries vs. Wets debate, extending that question to his chosen tackle makes sense, too. Was he fishing dry flies or wet? Most angling historians will tell you that, well . . . it depends. In the early twentieth century, American anglers, unencumbered by the hidebound debates over "proper" fly fishing techniques that had inflamed their overseas brethren, were free to float flies, sink nymphs, and pull streamers—so long as they caught fish. And in the Montana of one hundred years ago, catching fish never seemed to be an issue. In fact, it wasn't until 1928 that Montana Fish and Game got around to establishing a daily catch limit—a mere forty fish.

The water on this fine Sunday morning is still high on the banks, and the vegetation is young in its season. While full, the riparian band along the river is not yet overgrown. Indeed, the Drinking Fisherman seems braced for weather that's not cold but still a ways from the long, hot days of a Big Sky summer. Spring runoff has just ended. Longer days and warmer temperatures promise an early barrage of emerging bugs—perhaps the Mother's Day caddis hatch or an appearance of skwalas or stone flies. *Something* was going to pop.

Like today, one of those hatches was above all others—the famed salmonfly hatch. Known back then as a willow bug, the salmonfly is a big, clumsy insect that tends to skitter willy-nilly across currents and kicks helplessly in riffles, back eddies, and tailouts. Trout love to eat them. Anglers love to cast them.

Thanks to improving equipment, American dry fly fishing was coming into its own. And, like today, anglers were eager to see their flies gobbled on the surface. Popular dry patterns for the willow-bug hatch included: Willbur Beaty's Butte Bug, a body of woven orange floss under a wing of gray squirrel tail; Jack Boehme's Picket Pin, a flashy contraption wrapped in gold tinsel with a wing fashioned from gopher-tail hair; and the Missoula hometown favorite, the Bunyan Bug. Devised by Norman Means, this painted cork fly quickly became the go-to willow-fly pattern upon its creation in the early 1920s. Meanwhile, Tuttle's Devil Bugs, evil-looking creatures fashioned out of spun deer hair, were the rage among bass fishermen, and more than a few renegade trout fishers of the time adopted the Devil.

Our Drinking Fisherman could have mail-ordered his flies from the ubiquitous Sears catalog. Perhaps he sent off orders to the Weber Lifelike Fly Company of Stevens Point, Wisconsin; Lyon & Coulson from Buffalo, New

York; or L.L.Bean from Freeport, Maine. If he wanted to shop locally, he could have stopped at Bob Ward's Sports & Outdoors in Missoula. Opened in 1917, Ward's was owned by a Klondike gold miner who ran out of money on his way to Alaska. Instead of selling picks and shovels to miners, he sold guns, ammo, and fishing gear to Montana's hunters and fishers.

The Drinking Fisherman's rod is a sturdy stick joined by a staunch ferrule located in the center of the rod. Without a full view, we can only surmise that this was a two-piece rod. And if it was a two-piece, the next question becomes, was this even a bamboo rod? Maybe not. It could have been constructed of ironwood, ash, lancewood, or greenheart—materials that predated the artisanal four- and six-strip bamboo models but that didn't go out of mass production until the 1950s. With only two segments, the Drinking Fisherman's rod was nothing like the graceful, tactical buggy whips crafted by American rod-building masters like James Heddon, H.L. Leonard, and Everett Garrison—whose work today can reach into the thousands of dollars among collectors. No, this was a sturdy, utilitarian stick. A fishin' pole kept stashed in the truck for quick stops along Missoula's neighborhood streams like the Blackfoot, the Clearwater, and the Drinking Fisherman's beloved Rock Creek.

The Drinking Fisherman's reel is another curiosity. Note how it joins to the butt of the rod at an offset angle. This indicates the Drinking Fisherman probably employed one of the newfangled, side-mounted automatic models. Manufactured by a handful of companies at the time, automatic reels were marketed under names like the Mills Creek Whipper. They had the seemingly magical ability to retrieve line without cranking the spool. The cost in 1910? About $1.25.

Between 1910 and 1920, Missoula County had a population of about twenty-five thousand, roughly one hundred thousand fewer people than today. But even back then, Missoula was no backwater. The university was established in 1893, and the city boasted streetcars by 1910, a ballpark by 1911, and an airfield by 1913. So it is entirely within reason that the

Drinking Fisherman, enjoying a weekend away from his job at the university, could have motored the twenty-five miles east of town to hit the banks of Rock Creek, alongside a friend with a budding passion for snapping pictures.

In 1900, George Eastman introduced a revolution in photography: the "Brownie" camera, a simple, easy-to-use box camera that ushered in the concept of the "snapshot." In 1910, its price was one dollar. However, the Brownie captured its images on roll film, and we know that the Drinking Fisherman lives upon a 4-x-5-inch glass plate.

"This shot," says the Seattle-based photographer and angler Dave Perry, "is obviously the result of a very deliberate process. First, the composition is lovely. The photographer didn't just swing a camera and shoot this. With a 4 x 5 camera, you just didn't go out and snap off a roll of film. Each shot was framed very judiciously. Each shot counted."

These field cameras were by no means "point and shoot," nor were they compact. The heavy frame and bellows would have been set upon a tripod, emulsified glass negatives would have been loaded into the camera (in the dark!), and the shot would have been set up while the photographer stooped under a light-blocking black drape. "Remember," says Perry, "if it's a glass negative, he's probably only got ten exposures, and each one is a ten-minute process to get loaded into the camera. You really couldn't afford to mess up."

Classically composed according to the "rule of thirds," the picture appears to have been made using a wide-angle lens and a slow shutter speed, which underscores the depth of field and holds the focus of the photo from foreground to background. The light is luminously soft, almost glowing. No shadow is cast under the brim of the Drinking Fisherman's hat, and no flash creates stark tones upon his face. It is a well-crafted image capturing the start of a gorgeous day.

Of course, I didn't have to do all this digging to unearth the Drinking Fisherman's hows and whys. I've always understood him, always known him—the taste of beer upon the bank, a day bursting at the seams with possibilities, those gorgeous moments with friends before the serious, solitary work begins, caught within our own heads, answering the eternal critic at every fly selection, every cast. It's those louder, carefree moments on the bank—the moments so perfectly captured by the Drinking Fisherman—that we cherish as much as the times alone when we finally hook a trout.

It's almost too easy to say it, but we are, all of us, the Drinking Fisherman, joking and laughing beside the stream, trading stories, lies, and swigs of beer. We are also the Waiting Fisherman, bouncing on our toes, impatient, eager to march upstream and plunge into the flow—confident, tense, happy to be alive and fishing that stream, sucking in its cool, charged air on a stolen Sunday morning.

RIVER SONG

Three Walks in the Park

ONE

Put your head down and keep walking until you hit the river. It's about a mile. A straight shot from the road. Plopping-ant patterns along the bank will do just fine. Keep moving. Keep casting. Fish until the river begins to stink a bit—a fart in the waders a while back that went unnoticed? Or is there something dead around, because that would attract a bear, and that would be really, really bad. No. The smell permeates, rising from mud pots, fumaroles, and spooky portals in the earth's skin. Stink-steam everywhere. Somehow, the stream gradually becomes carbonated, and the riverbed transforms into something calcified and white, like freshly dried plaster. It's easy to lose your sense of time when the earth beneath your feet seems to have reverse-aged by billions of years.

Just where does the other trail come in? Decision time: turn back and follow the same path back to the truck or bushwhack across rutted bison trails, hoping to find the connecting trail? Swallow fear, begin bushwhack. Skulls, bison pies, scant tracks, but no trail . . . where the fuck . . . it was just here . . . gotta be here somewhere . . . keep walking . . . is that another hiker or is that a bear? When the actual trail is finally met, it is held in contempt—like it's been unfaithful, a liar. Return to truck, spitting and jabbing walking staff into the dirt.

TWO

Enjoy those last, leisurely moments at the trailhead. Better thought: Stretch out. Get limber. Gulp some water. Suck in fresh, clean air. This is a slog best traversed by strapping your gear down and blasting straight ahead for forty-five minutes. Look for bear to your north when you reach the first meadow. Enjoy the rolling hills and resist the urge to stop and fish. Yes, it looks like the best fly fishing in the world. It is mighty good. Actually, it's better than that. But don't stop. Remember, an angling pilgrimage to the second meadow will ensure a happy afterlife. It's only another forty-five minutes, and all the steep hills are in the rearview. Forward! One more thing, angler, keep an eye on the clock—it takes a while to get back, and no matter how good the fishing, you'd rather not spend a long night shivering in the first meadow with those grizzlies.

THREE

If you survive, every other riverside hike will appear as domesticated and safe as a pint of milk. Mud pots, stink holes, hell gates, earth scabs, crust blisters, geysers, fumaroles, lesions, and planetary abnormalities in a white, glaring light. The earth with a bad case of the bilious ague; humors all off; tremens delirium, or perhaps a lung-deep case of consumption, swirling with unseen spirochetes—a drip, drip, drip dosed with mercury and sulfur. Fishing ain't usually so bad, but for some reason the bastards didn't want adults, didn't want nymphs, and wouldn't take emergers. All shook, a terrible impoliteness. Alas, this is not a restaurant; you don't always get what you order. On the way out, Foghorn made the bad thing worse: "If we were any good—if we're as good as we think we are—we woulda figured out a way to catch them fish."

14

PLAN B

The Turneffe Atoll is Belize's wall of protection against the unrelenting tumult of the Atlantic Ocean. Storms, tides, and waves slap against this fragile portion of the world's second-largest barrier reef—pounding, irrigating, and feeding a 620-mile stretch of wilderness from the tip of the Yucatán Peninsula down to Belize, past Guatemala, traversing the Bay Islands of Honduras, and finally terminating east of Nicaragua. It is fine, vast, and untamed country that provides shelter to gamefish like tarpon, permit, bonefish, triggerfish, and more than five hundred other species, including mammals, birds, and reptiles. This sliver of the massive Mesoamerican Barrier Reef System allows the very existence of the Caribbean; it defines its perimeter and safeguards the sea's interior. It is a fecund, heady region—an immense aquarium that attracts anglers from everywhere.

Most of those anglers arrive with a plan. Curry and I have something like a plan—a mini, three-day plan. But after that plan, the plan is no plan—always a suitable plan. The destination is Belize, after all, and a skimpy non-plan feels like the right approach to take.

We land in Belize City, hop in a cab, and white-knuckle it to the deliciously funky marina. Two hours later, we are kicking it on the deck of a boat, beers in hand, puttering off to Turneffe Island Resort, a short skiff ride from the great reef. The sun is out, the weather is fine, and a DJ pumps dancehall music through the boat's scratchy PA. We have three days of guided fishing in front of us. The manager of the lodge has unequivocally promised us permit: "No problem, man. They're everywhere right now. Permit for days!" This seems reckless. Plans or no plans, you cannot promise a man a fish. Period. And a permit? C'mon.

Turneffe Island Resort is an ecolodge so lovely that I immediately feel out of place. It's a familiar sensation I get at fishing lodges—a few acres caressed out of the jungle or woods where everything is so lovely, so manicured, so cared for. The people at these sorts of lodges—guests and staff alike—are unfailingly friendly, have a healthy glow, and look freshly sexed, but I always feel like a dork just doing the simplest things—like walking around. I feel guilty, like everyone's in on my grift—a socially awkward fish bum masquerading as a writer and freeloading in paradise. It usually only takes a few beers to relax, regain composure, and recover from this feeling, but that line from the writer Thomas McGuane echoes in my head: "What things in life do you have to do to afford a bonefish trip?" Curry and I can't afford a bonefish trip. We are here on someone else's dime, so we pad around the grounds quietly, find our rooms, get our gear together, and try to avoid drawing negative attention.

⸻

The first morning of a fishing trip is always a shitshow—a hungover, blurry, queasy mess. But this morning is different. I feel spry. My gear is organized. I have energy. I am raring to go. This never happens because upon arriving at a fishing spot, be it a riverside campsite, high mountain lake, or plush Caribbean fishing lodge, I get excited and tend to overdo things the first evening. Not this time! It got dark and I went to bed. No dillydallying. For the first time in a decade, I'm in the rack and snoring by 9 p.m.

The sun wakes, and we swan around the boat dock in old flip-flops, grubby ballcaps, dingy sun shirts, and expensive polarized sunglasses. The lodge also caters to scuba divers. They eyeball us as we string rods, fuss over flies, and tie knots. We watch them squeeze chubby pink bodies into tight black wetsuits. Scuba—I get it. Nature. You are floating in it. It must be satisfying and probably very peaceful—the opposite of saltwater-flats fishing.

We push off and chug through the Belizean backcountry for thirty minutes, power down, and ease into the first position. In front of us, the open ocean pounds into the great reef, losing its ferocious power and trickling over the coral into the vast flats. Behind us is a labyrinth of mangrove creeks, islands, bays, and channels. Perfection.

I climb onto the deck, strip out line, and attempt to settle down and absorb the surroundings. It's tough to do both at the same time. It is so beautiful on these flats, but that beauty conceals brutality. Just below the surface, everything is hunting. Everything is hunted. Everything is killing. Everything will soon be killed. But still, it is so pretty, so lovely, so far from everything familiar. I take a few deep breaths, adjust my glasses, pull my hat down, and let out a casual flip to stretch my line and confirm I still remember how to cast. That first flip somehow lands on the nose of a permit. We both stare at the gently descending crab pattern, wondering what to do next. I have no idea. The permit is more certain. He disappears before I can capture a picture of the wavering fish in my reeling mind.

Permit come from nowhere, as if someone blew dust into the water and those particles coalesced into a fish that seems just barely there—a glint at the surface, a wavering below. As soon as that fish materializes, a ripple deconstructs it and it is gone as quickly as it arrived. It's nothingness we can almost grasp. I love how ridiculous and impossible this idea is.

I have three legitimate shots in the morning. I make three excellent casts right on the fish. No eats. What's surprising is, even into the wind, my throws are stiff and on target. That never happens. What is not surprising is that permit continue to be permit.

Curry climbs onto the deck. Back in Seattle, he works at a fly shop. He guides people for steelhead on the heroic rivers of the Olympic Peninsula. If anyone knows how to deal with failure, it's him. He is also very much like the guides here—like guides anywhere—unperturbable, inscrutable, patient, a secret-keeper.

I offer a back-of-the-boat thought to Curry: There is very little Zen to permit fishing. It is fast-twitch. Panic. Everything happening at once. There are shouted whispers. One cast. Two. Maybe three. That's all you get. Very little actual fishing is involved. It is hunt and stalk. Only occasionally does one get to fire the weapon.

Curry gets three quality shots in forty-five minutes. No eats. The fish don't react. They simply dissolve into that limitless nothing. He steps down from the platform and announces that permit fishing is bullshit. "I feel like with steelhead fishing, hooking a fish is just the icing on the cake," he says. "With permit fishing, the fish is the cake, the icing, and the cherry on top. Steelhead is more immersive. You are fishing all the time. You get locked in. You are part of the river."

"I see your point," I say. "But neither one of us has hooked one of these bastards yet, so we don't know. We can't know."

The words have barely fallen from my mouth when we both stop. A 6.5-foot, 350-pound manatee glides in front of the skiff. It is massive, and looks like it's been spackled together with bread dough. "Jesus," Curry gulps. "Never seen one of those on the Olympic Peninsula."

Turneffe Island is a buffet. We are fishing close to the great reef. In front of us, a hundred bonefish tails glint in the surf. It is a wonder. We exit the skiff and walk with them, casting, hooking a few but mostly in awe of this enormous herd, so casually grazing along this deserted, fragile sliver of a beach. We spend a couple hours with these fish, and then, as instantly as they've materialized, they disappear into the glare.

Back in the boat, we pole along the reef with an eye toward heading back to deeper water for permit, but then we see it—the thing—a brutalist heap of concrete and rebar known as the Belize Dive Haven Resort and Marina. It's as cozy as an airport terminal and sits on what used to be Ropewalk Caye, just yards from the delicate skin of the reef. There are tractors. We can see them digging a swimming pool and driving piles for the two-hundred-foot-long pier. How did this get here? Why is it here, in such a fragile place? Under construction since 2004, the site looks nearly completed but also strangely abandoned. (After fifteen years of tractors, backhoes, and pollution, the resort was opened in 2019.) I think of the McGuane quote again—just what did these people have to do in order to construct this thing?

The answer is not pretty.

The 96-room, 240-acre resort, owned by the Canadian eyeglass tycoon Sir Karim Hakami, is not popular with the locals—nor with scientists, anglers, and everyday humans deeply concerned about the conservation of the fragile reef ecosystem. The resort has blasted through the reef's coral to dredge a deep shipping channel allowing ingress and egress for large yachts and supply barges. The dredged material was used to fill mangrove and littoral forest to create new land. This has caused irreversible damage to prime habitat for conch, lobster, bonefish, permit, tarpon, and other species. It has also damaged the reef in front of the dredged area. The resort owners have hacked away the jungle and installed a landing strip. Brine from two desalinization plants is being dumped into a marshy area on the lagoon side of the property. This contaminates this area's soil and possibly the wider marine and reef ecosystem. And, planned for former mangrove and flats spawning grounds for gamefish is a new venue for tourists to motor out and buzz around on Jet Skis.

A report issued by the Turneffe Atoll Trust is a damning indictment of the economic and environmental impacts of the reef's development. Not surprisingly, its focus is the Belize Dive Haven Resort. "Environmental laws," the report concludes, "as well as important national master plans, have a direct bearing on development activities at Turneffe Atoll. However, in several cases these have been circumvented. A case in point is the Belize Dive Haven Resort and Marina."

Craig Hayes founded the Turneffe Atoll Trust in 2005. The owner of the eco-conscious fly fishing lodge Turneffe Flats since 1981, he's had a front-row seat to the development on Turneffe. "It's too late to turn down the damage," Hayes says. "The whole flat was dredged. The mangroves were cleared. That damage is irreversible. This will serve as an example of what should never be done again at Turneffe."

Hayes does not mince words when it comes to Belize Dive Haven: "It's a huge, ugly, out-of-place development that has done incredible damage to the environment of Belize," he says. "I've seen it now for years—the flat is gone. There is no flat anymore. The reef in front has been severely damaged. The shoreline they created is severely eroding. The mangroves are gone."

We pole past the resort. Everything about it is an eyesore. It simply doesn't belong, and seems an insult to the wild, vulnerable isolation of the Turneffe Atoll. Curry and I question our guide about the impossibility of this thing, but soon we run out of every question except "Why?" We glide away in silence.

After the sun falls, it's time for night fishing. We anchor the skiff in a deep channel a short run from the lodge. Warm breezes shush the bugs away. Our guide sweeps the mangrove banks with a bright-yellow beam, searching for the red dots of crocodile eyes. I lean back in the boat and take in the Milky Way. The tarpon are rolling under the moon and stars— some uncomfortably close to the boat. They jump, landing with a *kerploosh* that sounds like an anvil dropping into the water. This could have been a peaceful after-dinner float, but suddenly it's startling and a bit intimidating. Let's just say we tip over trying to land a fish. Fall in and we will be swimming around with tarpon, 'cuda, and sharks. If we make it to shore, the crocs await. The guide hands me a rod and I cast, swinging big, gaudy flies with the current, secretly hoping none of these enormous fish grab. What would happen then?

Our three days chasing permit (none), tarpon (none), and bones (some) have evaporated. The high-living, all-you-can-consume lodge plan has expired. There are no more free lunches. We are on our own, armed with lean wallets and high expectations. We have a week to do something—something else—somewhere in Belize. "So, what's the plan again?" I ask Curry.

"There is no plan, remember?"

We reluctantly shamble onto another boat and shuttle the thirty miles to the hustler's paradise of the Belize City Marine Terminal. From there, one can grab a cheap water taxi or bus to many exotic destinations. We have our pick: San Pedro, Honduras, Tikal, Long Caye. We choose Caye Caulker—a thirty-minute boat ride to a place with (allegedly) bonefish, beer, and a nice beach. Plan B.

It is blazing hot by the time we land and dump our gear in the shade on the town's main drag, Playa Asuncion. Old-school reggae is playing. A Rasta offers to sell us a baggie of brown ditchweed. He also lets us know he has coke, 'shrooms, and ecstasy—"for later." We drink water and then some beer. We need to find a cheap place to stay. Curry guards the bags, and I walk around until I find a small, tidy room. Bonus: they have a fleet of loaner cruiser bikes. Our no-budget non-plan seems to be coming together.

We find our room, plop down our bags, and walk around town. Knick-nacks, lobster dinners, T-shirts, scuba trips—it's all here. If you've got the money, ask and you shall receive. Curry and I turn down a side street where a line of guys sporting Hawaiian shirts, ball caps ,and sunburned calves stand in a queue. It's a pharmacy. They are buying six-packs of recreational Viagra. Curry and I opt for an unromantic evening eating nachos, looking at maps, and singing along with the cheesy classic-rock karaoke at an expat bar.

Belize unfurls in drama as the sun rises. That is no surprise. Dawn is beautiful almost everywhere. But when palm trees, gently lapping surf, and a day of fishy exploration are involved, morning seems so much better. We drink juice and water, get our shit together, and stumble into a delicious (and cheap!) breakfast-burrito shack just down the street.

Our first idea is to case the joint—get a feel for the terrain. We load up our packs and pick out our cruisers. Curry gets the first pick and chooses the finest steed. I'm stuck with one of the runts. It's okay, but it's no thorough-bred. Hell, it ain't even a plow horse.

There are only a few cars on Caye Caulker, but there are lots of golf-cart taxis, bewildered tourists, and dogs. We pedal south through the village, picking our way through conch shacks, snorkeling operations, and margarita bars. We stop at one of those bars and meet a French couple cuddling a rod tube and fishing pack. We chat. We exchange info. We look at each other's fly boxes. I don't have any of the gold and bronze bonefish flies that pack their box. Mine are all pink, like the ones used on Andros Island in the Bahamas. I feel a twinge of panic.

Caye Caulker is tiny. In minutes we are rid of the village and pedaling a singletrack along the beach. We roll south to a crumbling boat dock where a woman makes long, lovely casts into the ocean. It seems like something from a movie. We walk up the pier to find her throwing to a school of snap-per. But snapper, being snapper, keep cutting her leader. Curry ties up a wire bite tippet and gifts her some Clouser flies. In exchange, she draws us a map of the trail we are on, its major landmarks, its crocodile hangouts, and its course around this rollicking jungle sandbar set atop a coral ledge on the edge of the Atlantic Ocean.

It doesn't take long for the trail to get bad—really bad. It is overgrown and muddy. My bike chain keeps falling off. We have to get off and push through muck up to our calves. We lose flip-flops. We are sweating. We scan the jungle for crocs. Where do they hide? I expect one to come charging at me through the duff. It feels like we are doing something dumb and reckless.

Somehow, we make it to the first beach on our new map. It looks just fine. It's wadeable, with plenty of room and a nice tidal push. In the clearing, a group of workers stands knee-deep in the water. They hoist great armfuls of sea bottom into wheelbarrows. They are building a house for some anony-mous rich guy and taking their building material straight from the sea. It's backbreaking work, and all my bitching about the trail and my bike chain seems petty now.

We make small talk with the guys and put our rods together. As we are about to step in, suddenly, everyone and everything is in motion. The guys loading the sand move as quickly as possible, pumping their legs to get out of the water. Other guys are yelling. The dudes on the beach begin throwing rocks into the water. Then we see it. A huge croc, swimming with intent toward our clearing. I find a rock, as if it will defend me against a crocodile.

I don't really feel safe on the trail or the water, but since we don't see any more crocs, the next bay looks better than the first. I peel some line and wade in. Curry walks down the path a bit and wades in too. We walk and cast, cast and walk. I lose myself casting, scanning for fish, concentrating. Suddenly Curry is yelling. Imploring me to do something. "Get out of the water, man! Get out! C'mon! Quick!" I reel up and walk to the beach. Curry is ashen faced. "Crocs. Lots of 'em. Swimming all over the place," he says.

I've known Curry awhile. He's not really a kidder. He's calm—unflappable—but he has been flapped. We abandon our current plan and call it a day. It's Plan B time: beer.

We spend the next few days roaming the island, scanning off piers and boat launches, riding to deserted beaches looking for something to cast to and avoiding massive reptiles. We follow a fresh lead from a dreadlocked juice seller who tells us of some canals on the island's back side by the landing strip. Baby tarpon, he claims, flush the canals at daybreak and dusk. We push off through town, around the beach, and through the jungle to find the canals loaded only with bugs and frogs and sad piles of rubble and construction garbage. After a couple of hours of nothing, it is back to town, back to a big plate of chicken wings and a bucket of Belikin beer.

Caye Caulker is a magnet for expats, artists, backpackers, hippies, pleasure-seekers, beach bums, and assorted oddballs. While there is one established fly fishing lodge on the island, plenty of locals will load you into a panga and take you to the fish. Price is negotiable and often includes extras—Belikin, weed, lobster, jerk chicken; it's wise to negotiate creatively.

Curry and I finally break down and book a panga ride out to the flats with a guide named Vibes. It's a cheap day trip, and we aren't expecting much. But still, we are on a boat, we are going fishing, and Vibes is . . . entertaining. He says he's fresh from a six-and-a-half-year bit for drugs, or a fight, or a gun charge. I can't keep track. "I was a roughneck," he explains, "but now me settle down for me wife and baby girl."

Before visiting Belize, I did not know what a "square grouper" was, but Vibes fills me in. "It's my ticket, man," he tells me. "It's my way out. I find that bale and I don't tell no one. No one! I just lay low and build a nice house for my family."

This seems like a fair plan to me, so for the next few hours, when I am not scouting for bonefish, I pretend to help Vibes scour the mangroves for bales of coke or weed that may have washed up. I hope we don't find one. What would happen then? What's a Belizean prison like?

Vibes is distracted. We are not seeing any square grouper and we are not seeing many bonefish. Still, we manage to creep up on a few schools and get some shots, but somewhere, the French couple has all the good flies we forgot to pack, and the Belizean bones are much more intelligent than I anticipated. We check some abandoned lobster traps, troll for barracuda, drive the boat around, and finally admit it: Plan B sounds better than this plan.

Following another hot tip that night, Curry and I head down to the cut separating the sparsely populated north side of the island from the anything-goes south side. At dusk, our source informed us, big tarpon swim up the channel. Unfortunately, the tarpon cut is also the front lawn of a place called the Lazy Lizard. It is not a scene conducive to fly angling. All around us, the tan and the drunk whoop and shout-sing the choruses of songs by the Eagles, AC/DC, CCR, and Jimmy Buffett. We wade out, hoping to find some casting room, but there are hecklers, and suddenly I'm not into casting. Unless you are good friends with the hecklee, there should be no heckling in fly fishing. It can be disheartening.

Instead of joining our new pals Big Shawn, Boston Mike, and Dirtweed Dianne back at our favorite watering hole, Curry and I decide on a brand-new Plan B for our last evening. We will eat everything we can on the island until we run out of money. Together, we have $62. Plenty. We start with a delicious plate of lip-singeing jerk chicken on the beach. It is a fine appetizer for the lobster tails we tuck into only a few steps away.

We circumnavigate the town. We inhale a few sushi rolls at a beach bar. There is a greasy Chinese noodle joint. We rip into some fish-and-chips at a stand-up shop. Deeper into town, Curry settles into a plate of spicy stewed chicken while I mop up rice and beans and mac salad with a fried plantain under a fluorescent sign. We walk into a mom-and-pop and immediately order pig tails in tomato sauce. Somewhere along the way, conch is involved. Tomorrow we are scheduled to be on an airplane at 3 p.m. At least, that's the plan.

A Frazzled Constellation

Here's to that parachute Adams you plucked from your cowboy hat and gave to me on the banks of the Yakima. You called it "The Closer." It was lucky for me, too.

Jimmy gave me that ugly/beautiful cricket pattern. I miss Jimmy. We all do. I've never, ever fished that cricket. I've never fished that black-and-red bass popper, either. It's an ugly beauty, too—just like Jimmy's cricket. Here's to ugly flies that are beautiful, but mostly, here's to Jimmy.

Here's to the number 18 soft hackle that's now more a bare hook than an actual fly. Faded and lovely. It put the sneak on so many chunks on the Henry's Fork that night after the wind picked up and all the tourists went to dinner.

That's the muddler minnow you stepped on in the parking lot beside that little creek outside Durango, Colorado. You can have it back if you want.

Here's to the Clouser minnow whose eyes fell off but still tricked my first coho from the beach. I conked the coho on the head, slit it open, ate the salmon's still-beating heart, and saved the fly. That's it, right there. Still bloody.

The green butt skunk that fooled Julie's first steelhead got all rusted out in the drink holder. I finally threw it away two years ago. Sorry about that, Julie. It doesn't mean I don't love you.

That's the tiny caddis I had on when Lang hooked that poor, little swallow. After we untangled her and she flew away, I cut it off. I didn't fish the rest of that day.

The yellow-and-brown conehead broke a six-weight on Rock Creek. Luckily, I never did like that rod. On the way home that night, Montana Highway Patrol pulled me over on I-90 outside Missoula. The cop saw the swarm of caddis flies stuck to the visor and let me off with a warning even though I was driving on a suspended license and had two roaches in the ashtray. Here's to heavy flies that break shitty rods and to blind cops who'd rather talk fishing than write tickets—and to caddis flies stuck in the visor.

Here's to the three orange stimmies, three intruders, two hoppers, two caddis, two pheasant tails, two prince nymphs, one black woolly bugger, one crazy Charlie, one stonefly nymph, one kung fu krab, and one sex dungeon I have pulled, cut, or had someone yank out of various parts of my face and scalp, back, arms, fingers, and hands.

I never imagined a loony-looking purple haze emerger would ever catch fish, let alone a PhD rainbow on the Metolius. Thank you, Mister Haze, for one delicious, hard-won bit of glory on the toughest place to catch a trout in the Lower 48.

This truck has never been to South Andros, but that gotcha is from a guide who looked just like Biggie Smalls. He rolled joint after joint of weak Bahamian ditchweed and sang Marvin Gaye songs from atop the poling platform. From what I recall, it was an excellent trip.

This truck has never been to Alaska, but that's the dumb egg pattern that filled my freezer the winter I got fired, got divorced, and Willie the Wonder Dog got run over. I know that sounds like a country song, but it's mostly all true.

Here's to the gurgler those big-shouldered redfish hammered all day long with Jessie down in Port Aransas. I bought four at the fly shop but only used one. Go ahead and keep the other three. I know you got 'em, and I would have done the same thing. This is the only one I wanted back. Got it hanging from the rearview mirror now. It reminds me of you, ya thieving bastard.

I don't remember what the four two-fly rigs attached near the back window did, but it must have been epic. Why else would I take a two-fly rig out of the rotation?

There is plenty of love for the six chewed-up Quigley cripples scattered like a frazzled constellation across the roof liner. Even though a Quigley is my favorite trout fly, I've failed to keep track of why each of you resides in this hall of glory, but thanks for your service, unknown soldiers.

And here's to this self-healing, smelly, 1999 Ford Ranger in slightly faded green that's pulled these heroes across 242,345 miles, three sets of tires, a transmission overhaul, three brake jobs, thirty-one of the Lower 48, three provinces, and parts of Baja, Sonora, and Chihuahua—tolerant of cigarette smoke and resistant to beer, dog slobber, red-hot tears of regret, and home to approximately five dozen hall of fame flies in glorious repose.

ACKNOWLEDGMENTS

Fly fishing is built from indelible moments that we share with our adopted families. I would like to thank everyone who's gifted me countless moments and countless memories on and off the water: Kevin Green, Jim Leptich, Karl Schneiderman, Wyatt Thaler, Copi Vojta, Langdon Cook, and Riverhorse Nakadate—my oldest and closest fishing pals—these stories wouldn't exist without their shenanigans.

Langdon Cook, Miles Nolte, Wyatt Thaler, Riverhorse, and Lori Storts read early drafts and gave gracious advice and edits. Kate Rogers, Janet Kimball, Matt Samet, and the entire crew at Mountaineers Books had the vision, offered handholding, and did the heavy lifting to make this work come to life. Matt DeLorme dug deep to produce the breathtaking woodcuts that add soul to these words. Gratitude to Steve Sautner and John Larison for real-world publishing advice and to Mark Jordan for legal guidance.

Thank you to Jason Rolfe for giving fly fish literature a platform via Writers on the Fly and to Dave McCoy and Emerald Water Anglers for providing a home and building community for all those who fish around the Salish Sea. Jeff Galbraith at *Flyfish Journal* and my many comrades at Patagonia inspired me, mentored me, and shared their fearless creativity and passion.

Much respect to Kirk Deeter, Bryan Gregson, Earl Harper, Matt Smythe, Hal Herring, Chad Shmukler, Mike Sepelak, Cameron Scott, Joey Mara, Jeff Hickman, Mark Hieronymus, Chris Gaggia, AJ Gottschalk, Paul Puckett, Jon Tobey, Greg Fitz, Jay Johnson, Chris Hunt, Phil Monahan, and Tom Bie for helping me navigate the waters of the fly fishing industry.

I will never forget the late Larry Ragan. Thanks for teaching me to fish, boss. Always in debt to my Andrew Adam Newman for showing me how to be an editor, writer, and reporter and to Andy Hedden-Nicely for giving me a chance to exercise those skills.

Gibby, Madison, and Wendell, I love you. You were all very good dogs and patient fishing partners.

Lori Storts, thanks for your patience, your ideas, and for being the partner who makes coming home the best part of a fishing trip.

Finally, thanks to Sister Mary Whatshername, whose sheer ferocity and determination triumphed over unfocused rebellion and taught a fourteen-year-old punk kid how to type.

ABOUT THE AUTHOR

Steve Duda is a writer, editor, and musician whose work has helped shape the voice of fly fishing for more than three decades. Innovative, entertaining, and thought-provoking, his writing combines inventive language, far-flung adventures, and the moments of pure wonder that only fly fishing can deliver.

His essays, journalism, and opinion pieces have appeared in magazines including *The Drake, American Angler*, and *The Flyfish Journal* as well as in magazines and on websites in the United Kingdom, Europe, and Asia. He has been a featured reader for a number of Writers on the Fly tour events in addition to appearing in numerous films, podcasts, and interviews. His story "When We Get Together Again This Time Next Year" was adapted as a short film by Waist Deep Media. His story "Impossibly Violent and Savagely Fast" appears in the collection *Catch of a Lifetime*, edited by Peter Kaminsky. He spent eight years as editor of *The Flyfish Journal*—called "the cultural Bible of the sport of fly fishing"—renewing and revitalizing appreciation for the sport's venerable literary tradition while providing a haven for a generation of writers, artists, and poets.

Duda is head of Fish Tales at Patagonia, writing, editing, and providing creative insight for the outdoor brand's multimedia fly fishing team. Away from the water, Duda's cultural writing has been featured in *Rolling Stone* and the *Huffington Post* and on MTV and many other outlets. He lives with his partner, Lori, and a semi-feral feline/racoon hybrid named Kit he's teaching to play banjo.

MOUNTAINEERS BOOKS, including its two imprints, Skipstone and Braided River, is a leading publisher of quality outdoor recreation, sustainability, and conservation titles. As a 501(c)(3) nonprofit, we are committed to supporting the environmental and educational goals of our organization by providing expert information on human-powered adventure, sustainable practices at home and on the trail, and preservation of wilderness.

Our publications are made possible through the generosity of donors, and through sales of 700 titles on outdoor recreation, sustainable lifestyle, and conservation. To donate, purchase books, or learn more, visit us online:

MOUNTAINEERS BOOKS

1001 SW Klickitat Way, Suite 201 • Seattle, WA 98134
800-553-4453 • mbooks@mountaineersbooks.org • www.mountaineersbooks.org

An independent nonprofit publisher since 1960

YOU MAY ALSO LIKE: